BY Millie L. McGhee-Morris

Published by: New Writers in Action

Shocking Truth Lies

©2018 by New Writers in Action ISBN: 978-0-9890957-8-5 ISBN 52799 $27.99

LCCN Imprint Name: **Havre De Grace, Maryland**

Publisher: New Writers in Action Inc.

Editors: Bonnie Quin/Patrice Brown

Book Cover Design and Layout by Gerry Norris art.mamaroneck@minutemanpress.com

"You can do whatever you set your mind to do if you really want it bad enough." -Millie

Dr. EGIESEDER ☺

Thank you

enjoy

Author's Book-Signing Page ☺

Millie M.

Millie L. McGhee Morris_

www.milliemcgheemorris.com

Note: This book was done from start to finish under the direction of Millie L. McGhee-Morris. She felt she needed to write and publish this work herself. So, if there are any errors in spelling, grammar, or the design; she apologizes for any inconvenience. Please understand that Ms. Millie was self-taught after finishing high school illiterate. She wanted this work to reflect her work alone. She was 10 years old when this story was told to her, and now she is 71 years old. She prays that you enjoy this work! ☺

Shocking Truth Lies

"The Truth about Two Families"

The **Me Too movement…** (**#MeToo movement**), is a movement against sexual harassment and sexual assault.

*Now, Millie, "**In Honor**" of all the women…*

Especially the three slave women, Sarah, Elizabeth, and Emily! They were raped, sexually incest by their slave owner, half-brothers, cousins and family's male friends. Those women were Millie's generational grandmothers; her "(4th) Great-great-great-great, - (3rd) great-great-great, and (2nd) great-great grandmothers."

We can also say with Millie #MeToo: for those listed below in Millie's family -

> ➢ My Ancestors!

> ➢ My Descendants!

> ➢ My Mother!

> ➢ My Sisters!

> ➢ My Nieces!

> ➢ My Daughter!

> ➢ And Millie! - **#me too!**

Contents

Dedication

I dedicate this book to my husband Dr. Leslie L. Morris for supporting me all these years, and finally, to these people I had in my life when I needed them:

- ➢ Tyara M. Reed, (Played Little Millie in the Documentary)
- ➢ Jonathan and David Mouton
- ➢ Big Daddy, "Clarence Allen."
- ➢ Mother, "Alberta Allen McGhee."
- ➢ Father, "Rev. Wm. McGhee."
- ➢ Historian Lucius Bowser
- ➢ Historian Julian Burke
- ➢ Historian Tam Tenpenny-Lewis.
- ➢ Historian George Ott, and assistant Ted
- ➢ FBI Special Agent M. Wesley Swearingen
- ➢ Lydia McGhee-Mouton
- ➢ Journalist Larry Carroll
- ➢ Public Relation: Mertine Moore Brown
- ➢ Journalist Dr. Barbara Reynolds
- ➢ Reggie and June Mckenzie
- ➢ Kristy Hoover and Daughter Haley
- ➢ Danny Arguello

Acknowledgement

Thanks to my lovely parents, William and Alberta McGhee for being supportive in every way possible, although our mother has passed on. Special love and thoughts in memory of Lucius Bowser, and Julian Burke. Special thoughts to the memory of my Big Daddy, Clarence Allen, and Big Mama, Lydia Allen. May they rest in peace!

Acknowledgment of the love for our blended family, my grandchildren: Bryan Morris, Jeremiah Morris, Tyara Reed, Chase Morris, Thomas Budris, Mala Morris, Noah Budris, Nelson Morris, Ava Reed, Troy Reed, and great-granddaughter Aryn Thomas, Nyla Brown, Nola Brown, and Nikki Brown.

Special love and thanks to our adult children that we share, Kymberly Reed, Vincent Reed/Cheryll, Christopher Morris/Shelia, Kevin Morris, Leslie Morris Jr., Lauren Budris. Aaron Brown/ Teresa, for loving me.

Many thanks to the following people who were always supportive and caring during this journey in my life: Cousin Diana Butt, Alexis, and Rodney Lynk, my sisters—Queen, Lydia, Sylvia, Julia, and Jeannette—

Special thanks to these wonderful people, family, and friends who have always supported this work during events and financially supported: Reggie and June McKenzie, Tamela Tenpenny-Lewis, George Ott, AAHGS National, AAHGS Arkansas, and in loving memory of all my ancestors.

-Author Millie L. McGhee-Morris

Foreword

It's a great pleasure to write the foreword in this book on behalf of my dear friend for more than a decade, which is long overdue.

"The will to do, the tenacity to overcome all obstacles and to finish the course, the strength to cling to inexorable ideals, are all rooted in courage".   -J. Edgar Hoover

Little did J. Edgar know when he spoke those words that he would be describing his third cousin Millie L. McGhee, author of Shocking: Truth Lies. This book closes a door that has remained open far too long with whispers and rumors of *J. Edgar Hoover-Passing for White?*

Tenacity to overcome obstacles?   Growing up in the segregated state of Mississippi, raised in poverty in the plantation town of McComb, and graduating with functional illiteracy, overcoming obstacles became a pattern in the life of our author. Although Millie learned early on that she had an entrepreneur spirit and her compassion for helping others she lacked the academic education to achieve her goals. So, what did she do next?

She finished the course!   After graduating high school Millie moved from McComb, Mississippi to Los Angeles, California. Determined to overcome the humility of a substandard education Millie acquired a personal tutor, attended classes at city colleges, and took classes in private schools. Over the next 21 years, she exercised the philosophy that she taught to others; *"that they could do anything they set their minds to if they truly believed in themselves"*.

From this philosophy, she established literacy programs, academic scholarships, entrepreneurship training and a platform for unpublished writers to become published authors.

Upon our first meeting, I was captivated by her tenacity and ambition to succeed. I was impressed that this small bundle of fire who fought her way through illiteracy and humble beginnings had become this successful entrepreneur, philanthropist, and author.

However, what brought us together more than two decades ago was the call of Millie's deceased loved ones. The spirits of the Allen and Hoover ancestors would keep their silence no longer. The time had come for the truth to be told and the record set straight on the identity of J. Edgar's ancestry. Exposing this truth would release the restless souls of Uncle Ivery and Mozilla, who lost their lives by daring to share the family secret, allowing them to finally rest in peace.

Called upon to answer the call, Millie enlisted the help of family, friends, genealogists, and historians to document the truth and expose the lies of J. Edgar Hoover's ancestry. This support allowed her to document the connection between the Black Allen's and White Hoovers and unlock the memories of the past that she had buried in her subconscious so long ago.

As a friend, I know the path laid out for her by those that came before has been a difficult and unfavorable journey. Many have disputed her writings, calling it fiction, fantasy, and oral history not substantiated. But what this book will reveal is ***the strength of Millie L. McGhee to cling to inexorable ideals,*** remaining steadfast in honoring the desires of her ancestors. These ancestors watched over Millie during this 21-year journey, keeping her ***rooted in courage*** as she completed *Shocking Revelation; J. Edgar Hoover & Mildred L. McGhee-Morris.*

12

To the reader, whether you believe the history or not, you should be inspired to follow the journey to your past. The better you know those that came before you, the better you will come to know yourself, enjoy the journey!

It would be remiss of me to begin this forward with a quote by J. Edgar and not end with one.

"It can be held certain that information that is withheld or suppressed contains truths that are detrimental to the persons involved in the suppression."
-J. Edgar Hoover

Tamela Tenpenny-Lewis
Genealogist/Historian/Cemetery Preservationist
Past National President, (AAHGS) Afro-American Historical & Genealogical Society, Inc.
Co-founder, Preservation of African American Cemeteries, Inc.

Prelude

THE SPIRIT OF ANCESTORS

Millie was inspired and ready. She sat down in her office that day with a view from her window of the blue sky, and green droopy hanging trees that swayed across her window when the wind blew. She began to talk to God and made a promise as she closed her eyes to have a conversation with Him. She expressed thanks to Him for trusting her with the family secret at such a very young age and for protecting her family from harm. She also believed God had a plan all along for her life, which was the reason those secrets were placed into the pitch-dark corner of her mind for many years so Millie couldn't see it. It was a hiding place for the secret to protect Millie and her family. Her father was a Baptist Minister and always told her this, *"What's done in the dark will come to light."* So, the ten years old girl was placed in His care as His holy vessel to hold on to this darkness until the time of His choosing. Millie believed the call for that door to open for her to get ready to do His will and unleash this family's secret into the world was now.

Millie was a free-spirited and happy little girl. She was more mature than most ten-year-olds her age. Like most kids her age, Millie knew everything and nothing, all at the same time.

She delighted in asking questions. A proud retort was no surprise from Millie. If she knew the answer, Millie was sure to speak up and tell it, just as she did one day in history class when a boy's questions sparked a distant memory that led her to a conversation with her Big Daddy, she has never been able to forget. Her entire life changed that Sunday afternoon. All she wanted that day was for her grandfather to assure her that what she knew was correct, but she got more than that from him that day. Millie learned more than her pre-adolescent brain could process from her Big Daddy that day.

Decades later, she accepted the responsibility she came to understand would be her charge —to share how living with secrets in a family preserves the curse leaving future generations to cope with the damage of those lies.

Millie didn't understand how the internalization of the information given to her by her Big Daddy and mother had affected her life as much as it did in the years that followed. Family reunions were no longer pleasant. The mere thought of attending them filled Millie with anxiety. In the weeks before the family reunion, she would begin to think about saving her family from being killed by the threats made by J. Edgar Hoover. She would find herself trying so hard to push those thoughts deep inside and lock the door.

She wanted those memories gone, because, during the time of family reunions that was to be a celebration of family bonding, she could only think about the many people around her who potentially knew bits and pieces of what she'd known for decades. Millie soon found it hard to look anyone in the eyes for fear that in theirs she'd see the distance that separated them from their real family history or in hers they would know the pain of her private struggle with her individuality as a black woman in America. An America that made it possible for one person's skin to matter in one way and others' skin to matter in another.

Millie had spent years consumed by the injustices that were still obvious despite the proclaimed progress that had taken place in America since the slavery days, which forever harmed her family, had ended for them. However, the harms of our past find new places in our present.

Before and after the reunions, Millie recalled what her Niece had revealed to her in 1990 about the sexual incest she had endured from her father, uncles and other older men in the family. The thought of that day when her Niece bravely shared the information to free herself to embrace her future as a wife and mother, Millie would be sickened to think of all the time she held inside memories that had stolen her innocence and her youth. Like Millie, her mind was aging while her heart got stuck at age 7 or 9 when incest broke it. What happens in the dark will surely come to light. She was not the only one. Other women and girls in the family had endured the same. Some in the present moment could tell vivid stories of their sexual ordeals with family members they knew were not appropriate, and for that very reason, others in their family had done it, they too kept it secret.

It was clear, many cousins, aunts, sisters, uncles, and even nephews kept secrets. Millie saw many at family functions that could be hiding behind a mask of shame cast upon them by the family curse that had survived hundreds of years. Their secrets, like the secrets of their ancestor's, may have been captured in photos, videos, and other artifacts their children and their children's children will look at hundreds of years from now and have no idea. That is right, "No idea, who did what to whom or what secrets each person took to their grave."

This book in your hand has the documents of the journey to personal freedom for Millie. Finally, she let go – of the past, the secrets, the pain, and the memories. Now in her seventies, she was comfortable enough in her own mulatto brown skin to express more clearly what she was supposed to do. She followed decades of genealogical work, traveling, and researching to trace her family history. A history that would lead both to fame, per J. Edgar Hoover who was the infamous Director of the FBI, and the pain, seen through Sarah, Elizabeth, and Emily the three slave women. And so many others who lived in the wake of others' abuse of women and their bodies to create a world that was "real" only to themselves; who were the men of evil spirits? Yes, it's true!

Now, Millie is the storyteller writing down her thoughts into this book from her childhood for the world to see. She had lived a life threatened by this secret for years. It overwhelmed her and caused depression as she suffered in silence, as she hid these secrets inside creating broken relationships and emotions so strained that surely could have taken her desire to live.

Interestingly enough, she kept her promise to her Big Daddy and never mentioned the secret to anyone as a child. Now, nearly five decades after J. Edgar Hoover was not of this world she started writing down her thoughts. Millie said a lot of her memory was pouring into her mind from her ancestors. Now in 2019, she is ready to tell the entire world the family's secrets that affected her life. This book is not just about J. Edgar Hoover living his whole life in secret, but also about the two murders in the family, and those three slave women that suffered the sexual abuse for decades to protect their half/white children including J. Edgar Hoover. She now wondered how much of the mainstream public knew that J. Edgar Hoover was the grandson of a slave woman. Millie's detailed hard work has compelled her to shine a light into the past to find the shocking truth and lies that connected her family to J. Edgar Hoover's family and their ancestors.

Millie did some serious thinking about the writing of this book and she believes that this book should not dwell only on J. Edgar Hoover's circumstances because it would be a mistake, due to what she discovered hidden deep inside of her family tree.

"There is was a generational curse of sexual incest in our family." A family member said.

Millie thinks J. Edgar was a sleaze bag for the awful things he did to her family with his threats to kill them if they disclosed his secret. She believed, *"J. Edgar was a child who fooled himself."*

She thinks the real culprit in the family history was Christian Hoover who was a minister, a legislator, and a Mississippi plantation owner, who owned over 100 slaves.

The 16-year-old girl Sarah that was brought out of West Africa had no name that Millie knew of; she just noticed her name in the research as a slave woman living on the Allen plantation. Millie also heard that name as a child but didn't know where Sarah fit into the Allen family history tree and said,

"Maybe Sarah is the name of the 16-year-old that was taken from Africa, Aunt Lillian Haynes talked about her at our family reunions for years."

Christian Hoover prepared a living-will before he died giving the plantation and slaves to his son William Hoover born in 1832. One of those slaves that was willed to his son was soon a bed-warmer for him, his brother, and their friends.

Millie came to realize that this book needed to start with the three African-American women who had struggled with sexual incest by their father, cousins, and their friends of the slave owners. Millie thought this history within the

Hoover and Allen Plantations was entirely different from what she had studied regarding slavery in her lifetime. Why? It was because it appeared to Millie to be operated for the pleasure of the slave owner, his sons, and their friends.

Millie heard the men storytelling as she hid under the porch playing a game called 'Hide and go seek' at the age of sixteen with her cousins. The men were speaking of the sex money playing games that the slave masters had invented that took place in the barn. The slave owners invited other slave owners to participate by placing bets on two slave couples having sex, and they called it, "The First Climaxing Game."

Millie had a flashback of her niece who had come to the family to tell what had happened to her at 14-years-old. When she went to the family to confess she said,

"I believe there was a "Generational Curse" in our family and it is still going on today, which is called, "Sexual Incest" in our family."

Millie's Niece was in her early 20's at this time, and she told the family that she came to them not because of what had happened to her because she felt like a nasty little girl. She thought it was a "Generational Curse of Incest" in the family. This young family member just wanted the curse to be 'STOPPED,' to protect her sisters, cousins, and also other children. Millie was saddened to hear her niece feel like this was all her fault. That goes to show you how many women get sexually abused/incest by a family member and feels as though it's their fault. She felt like she was a nasty little girl for allowing her own father to introduce her to sex; telling her, "This was what all fathers do with their daughters to introduce them to sex at an early age." Millie said she broke down and cried her heart out, to think a brother of hers and a father would do this to his child. It hurt Millie to the core.

Millie said, "My brother and all men that have that impulses should read in God's word, "Exodus 34-7" it is a pattern of sin to sexually abuse your child. The bible says, "God punishes the children and their Children for the sins of the father into the third and fourth generation."

Millie's niece had said there is a curse in the family. When she said that back in 1990, Millie decided then to set out on her mission to find the truth of where the Curse begin." Unbeknownst to her, this was opening up all those hidden secrets that were lying hidden in the corner of her mind.

That's when Millie started researching within the family, and she couldn't find anything in 1990. However, the nightmares began again soon after her marriage to Dr. Morris. Millie disclosed to her husband that she was having reoccurring nightmares that had been haunting her since her 27th birthday and she was 44-years-old. Millie's husband is a psychiatrist, and after he heard the details surrounding her nightmares, it was clear to him she needed psychological help to decipher her dreams. So, he arranged for her to get help, and by 1997 after seven years of therapy, Millie was ready to do some digging into the past to find that "Curse." Her husband told her she was like a zombie working night and day for hours to find her roots. She was up all night looking through documents she had found because she had made it her passion to find the truth.

Then when Millie found the history that documented the incest regarding the true-life story of those three slave women in the Allen and Hoover family's record; **Sarah, Elizabeth**, and **Emily** on her family tree, she saw the Curse. Then Millie said,

"If that wasn't incest and a Plague in our family that started from the beginning of our lives back to 1796. I don't know what else to say."

Millie's niece was *right on the money*; that they had a 'Generational Curse' in the family that came from slavery.

Millie's Mississippi roots and J. Edgar Hoover's Washington, DC roots, came to life that day in 1957 when Millie was only ten years old and she was in a history class in McComb, Mississippi.

Chapter 1

HISTORY CLASSROOM

This was a cold, dreary day in mid-April, the sun was barely up, and Millie didn't feel happy about going to school. She lived in the southern part of the country, which was Mississippi. People didn't say, "The sun was shining," they would say, "*The sun is up.*"

In 1957, Millie was as happy as any ten-year-old girl could ever want to be up until that one April day sitting in a classroom having a discussion that would later be the very foundation that opened up "Pandora's Box."

Millie got into an argument with a classmate in her history class about a man nobody in that part of the world liked or knew much about. So she thought. The students were in the middle of studying in class about the presidents of the United States when a boy named Lamar proclaimed,

"J. Edgar Hoover is the president!"

Millie began to wonder to herself where she'd heard that name Hoover in her life. In a flash, she remembered. Her grandfather, "Big Daddy" and her mother had told her stories about their ancestors who were slaves and that the Hoover family owned them. History was one of Millie's favorite subjects, and she had no doubt that she knew J. Edgar Hoover was in the Federal Bureau of Investigations (FBI), and not the president, so she said,

"What's wrong with you Lamar? That Hoover man is in the FBI, and he is not the president. We are studying the US presidents today, just in case you didn't notice."

The teacher, Mr. Gatlin, was not amused with them fighting in class but impressed with Millie's knowledge of what position J. Edgar Hoover held. He listened to their debate for a few moments, before quietly referring them back into the lesson,

"Now students, we must stop this argument and get back on the subject of United States Presidents."

Millie noticed Lamar making faces toward her, growing pleased with his ability to upset her; his behavior only increased her displeasure with being a jerk. Besides, it was both misleading and counterproductive for him to think that way. She thought for him not to understand the correct history of this Hoover man, who was not the Presidents, would be awful for him going forward. Mr. Gatlin caught him making faces at Millie, and he said,

"Listen, just to be clear on the subject of this debate between the two of you, J. Edgar Hoover is not, and has never been, president of the United States. So, now with that said, Lamar and Mildred, we are going to move on to the subject that we are studying today."

That was fine with Millie, and she smiled, *(her face showed justification)* at Lamar, and he didn't like that at all. Suddenly he jumped up and said,

"Well! He has more power than any president!"

That statement annoyed Millie because she knew this man and wondered if Lamar knew him as well. So she said to the teacher,

"Mr. Gatlin, I'm wondering if Lamar knows the difference between an FBI agent and the President of the United States?"

Mr. Gatlin realized Millie was serious about her history and wanted Lamar to be clear, so he showed her support and spoke openly to Lamar,

"Lamar, Mr. Hoover is the head of the FBI and has nothing to do with the President's job. So, can we move on to our lesson for today?"

Unfortunately, that didn't stop Lamar from his belief of J. Edgar Hoover having greater power than the President, so he stood up then, and said,

"He has more power than the president. I can see that myself! He runs the country doesn't he?"

This was becoming increasingly obvious that Lamar was not going to give up. Mr. Gatlin and Millie tried once again to help him understand that he was on the wrong track. Then, Mr. Gatlin explained,

"Lamar, that may be what a lot of people think, but you need to know that J. Edgar Hoover is not running this country, and furthermore Lamar, we are not going to discuss the subject any further today. It ends now, okay?

Lamar was not happy about the debate ending, but he nodded his head to the teacher and slumped down in his chair trying not to glance at Millie. It was also apparent that he had been listening to the adults in his family. Many people saw J. Edgar Hoover as a mighty powerful man, and so did Millie's family.

The only difference was that Millie's family knew of his secret, and his threats, which was why he felt the need to appear to be so controlling during his lifetime.

After that class, Millie could hardly wait to get to Big Daddy's house to talk to him. Millie had heard the name Hoover as a family connection during their family reunions since she could remember. She wanted to be clear about how the Hoover family related to them.

Millie believed that Big Daddy knew just about everything about anything. He was her tall hero, and a handsome light-skinned man that Millie thought was seven feet tall.

She was anxious and needed to get to see him as soon as possible. She loved going to his house, and as a child, she thought he lived out in the country because of the long ride from her home to visit him. She also noticed the size of the big white house sitting off from the road.

Millie enjoyed seeing her Big Daddy sitting up high on the porch that wrapped around the front of the house. She thought it looked like a mansion that only the white people could own. It made her feel like they were famous people in the town. Little that she knew they were because everyone knew her grandparents since Big Daddy was a carpenter who built many of the homes in the community.

Big Daddy was married to Big Mama who was a strong spirited woman, as most of the black women were back in that time. Millie was afraid of her, because she was bossy, and bossed everyone. However a good woman, she was well known in her church and a member of the Eastern Star organization.

The Eastern Star organization was a way of survival for black people. It was and still is a masonic appending body opened to both men and women. Millie's father was a member of the Mason organization, and her mother was a member of the Eastern Star. It was an exciting organization that was established in 1850 by a lawyer. He was an educator named Rob Morris, a noted Freemason that wasn't adopted nor approved as an appending body of Masonic Fraternity until 1873.

http://www.masonicdictionary.com/oes.html

There are many reading this book would question this statement, *"Big Mama was a strong spirited woman, as most of the black women were back in that time."*

Well, Millie had her views on the statement, she felt it was because the men gave them the position to run the house because many of the men were uneducated and the black-women used their motherly instinct to take care of the household.

When Millie arrived home after school, Millie found her mother and father in the kitchen cooking dinner and talking about her father's sermon. Her mother was a tall small-framed woman and very pretty, who was always quiet and reserved around people in the church. However, she was quite vocal at home keeping order running their household. Millie's father trusted her to take care of the home because though he was a pastor, his education was also limited. He was pastoring more than three churches, and the members didn't know of his illiteracy, because he had memorized the Bible.

Millie's Mother worked as a seamstress around the house humming and singing; she designed clothes for the ladies in the community. She designed an outfit for Jimmy Rogers once. Millie's mother was a seamstress by trade, and her husband was a minister, they had ten children, almost as many as their parents.

As Millie entered the house after school, she was still thinking about that history debate, and she found both of her parents as usual in the kitchen. So, Millie excitedly entered and said,

"Mom and Dad, can I please ask a question?"

They both stopped talking. Millie's parents felt she has something important to talk about on her mind because her eyes showed fear, she couldn't stand still, and she acted quite nervous.

Her mother or father didn't call her Millie that was her nickname and her mother replied,

"Yes Mildred, you may ask."

This made Millie happy, being able to talk to her parents about her history class. She proceeded to tell them about her day,

"I learned something in my history class today about a man named Hoover, and I want to ask Big Daddy about it. So, when can we visit him?"

They turned and looked at each baffled about what was troubling their daughter about the Hoover name.

"What is it, Mildred? Maybe we can help?"

Millie's father asked using a very reassuring tone to let her know that he wanted to help, and that surprised her. She was secretly hoping that she hadn't offended him by asking to talk to Big Daddy.

Right then, the sheepish and pensive look on his face meant Millie needed to tell him why she wanted to visit and talk to her grandfather.

Millie nervously explained,

"I had an argument in my history class about a man named Hoover who works for the FBI. Lamar, who is my classmate, said Hoover was the President. I told him that he wasn't. I wanted to ask Big Daddy more about the Hoovers who owned Grandmamma Emily."

Millie's father's face relaxed a bit. A faint smile replaced the mild wrinkle in his brow. Millie could tell that her father was proud of her for having the desire to know more about their history.

Her father waited a moment before walking over to Millie to say it was all right, and they would take them all to visit on Sunday. Millie was excited. She couldn't wait to go out to the country to the big white house that she loved so much. Sunday couldn't come fast enough for her.

Sunday finally came, and Millie's household was in a whirlwind of excitement. While everyone clamored about getting ready for the road trip, Millie knew she had to wait her turn to get into the bathroom. The apartment seemed unusually small particularly that morning, compared to their Big Daddy's big white house. She wondered how they all fit into the little apartment with nine children. Even more, she started to think about them all fitting into the car that only had five seats, and especially when they went on long trips to Big Daddy's house.

Her father had strict rules about the girls being fully clothed before leaving their bedroom. So, she had to wait her turn to get into the one bathroom.

This was one of the happiest days of Millie's life. It was a great day, the sun was shining, and the big green trees all around the house had big leaves that helped to shade the play areas outside. It was always great to visit and listen to their storytelling regarding the good old days. Millie was finally there, and ready to learn more about the Hoover family connection to the Allen family.

Chapter 2

BIG DADDY'S TALK

This day started with the sun shining, it was a beautiful day, no clouds in the sky. Millie was hoping for sunshine because she always loved to sit out on the porch under Big Daddy's legs and listen to storytelling.

Big daddy's house was miles apart from any other home. We were going down a long curvy road in the rough backwoods of McComb, Mississippi. There stood a big white house with long banisters and high steps that lead from the driveway to the porch. And on that porch sat Big Daddy, just like always, in the corner of the porch with his long legs stretched across the banister, smoking his pipe. Millie was happy it didn't rain that day, and to see her Big Daddy sitting looking so relaxed.

As they were getting out of the car, Millie jumped out and took off running, and ran up the high porch steps to Big Daddy. She sat her small body under his legs as if she was hiding. They all could smell Big Mama's food; the fried chicken, greens, rice and gravy; yams, fried squash, and cornbread that she prepared for them every Sunday when they came to visit. Big Daddy noticed little Millie hiding under his legs, and smiled down at her and said, "Hello, little one, what's on your mind today?"

She was excited, and out of breath from running, she couldn't speak for a moment, but when she finally could, she said,

"Hi, Big Daddy! I love you so much, and I have something I want to talk to you about today!"

Millie remembered, Big Daddy didn't say much, but when he talked, everyone listened. Smiling down at the excited little girl looking excitedly back at his feet, he removed his pipe and said,

"Okay, what is on your mind today my child?"

She just jumped right into it and said,

"I was in history class this past week studying the presidents of the United States, and Lamar, that's a boy in my class; said that J. Edgar Hoover was the president and I told him that was not true."

Big Daddy was looking at her with concern in his face when he heard the name Hoover, and quickly replied,

"What you told him was correct my child."

What he said made her feel great! So, she said,

"Big Daddy, Lamar then replied to the teacher that J. Edgar Hoover had more power than the president of the United States, and I was not happy with what he said."

Big Daddy again had a look on his face that Millie had never seen before; it was a deep thought look, then he replied,

"Well, that could be the true child. Mr. Hoover does have a lot of power. So, little girl what else do you want to know today?"

Millie was sensing something different from Big Daddy. She took a moment to think about his question to her but felt she might be crossing the line, but she had to know, so, she just quickly blurted it out,

"Is J. Edgar Hoover a part of the Hoovers who owned great, great grandmother Emily?"

He didn't answer right away, and slowly removed his pipe from his mouth, shrugged his shoulders up and down, and carefully came out with these words, saying,

"That old goat is my second cousin!"

Millie couldn't believe it! She began to get excited, Mr. Hoover was a famous man, and she had just been told that he was related to their family! Millie's heart was jumping out of her chest with excitement! However, Big

Daddy knew his little girl, inside and out! He could tell she was itching to let everybody know that she was related to someone important and famous. Then Big Daddy became very serious with her, and she was a little taken back. He didn't look all excited like she thought he ought to have been. No, he was earnest with her. He said,

"Now I don't want you to go telling anyone that he is related to us. This is a family secret that stays only in the family. This man doesn't want to be a part of us."

Big Daddy Why?" Millie asked, and she continued,

"I don't understand why we should keep his secret?"

Big Daddy's answer was even more severe than it was before, in a very rough tone, he replied,

"You Listen! I said don't you tell anyone what you heard here today! It wasn't my intention to tell you that information. That man doesn't want anyone to know that he is a part of this family!"

Big Daddy was starting to frighten Millie.

"Listen, J. Edgar Hoover is passing for white," he explained.

Big Daddy was not getting through to her, and he knew it. He looked right into her eyes with that look that told her he could see clear through her soul, and then he said,

"You Listen to me if you tell anyone, J. Edgar Hoover will have us all killed as we sleep."

Millie's knees began to shake, but her Big Daddy wasn't done yet.

"We all could be burned to death in our beds if you speak of any of this secret to anyone," he said.

Millie was just shocked at what he was saying to her, and with tears in her eyes, she asked,

"Would he do that to us Big Daddy?"

He replied,

"Yes, my dear he would. This man doesn't want to be known as a "Negro." Remember, he is a powerful man, and could have us all killed!"

Then she asked,

"Big Daddy why do you believe that he would have us all killed?"

That was the ultimate question, and the answer that he gave her was a good reason for the entire family to be afraid. His reply was so detailed and graphic as if he was telling a story out of a novel. Although Millie understood, he didn't want her to know any more of the secrets, because he felt she was still too young. Since he had blurted out the secret to her, he thought he had to tell her the reasons why she had to keep the secret too. He also knew she was very inquisitive for her age. Even at that age family members thought of her as nosey. Of course, she didn't agree, and she loved family history and knowing about her roots was essential to her. The story Big Daddy told her finally shut Millie down, and she never spoke of this secret to anyone for the safety of her family. The story was sad, and the horror of it pierced into her heart. She could see the tears in his eyes as he began to speak more of the story to her, as he continued,

"Well, this is why I feared for our family's safety and believed the exact words that old goat, J. Edgar said. He would have us all killed if anyone told his information. His half-sister and biological father were both murdered trying to convince him to claim his heritage and embrace both sides of his family, "The Black and the White-side." We believed that he was in a powerful position to be able to change a lot of hatred in the world and help bring the Negro race and the White race closer without hatred."

Millie interrupted him and asked,

"Why would J. Edgar Hoover think that admitting he was a "Blackman" in his position could change the hatred?"

Big Daddy replied,

"Daughter J. Edgar knew how much white's hated blacks, and he felt it would get him killed if anyone found out that a black man was running the FBI. It was clear to us that J. Edgar wanted us to continue keeping his secret since it had been a secret since he was born. It was other secrets kept during the time our great-great-great grandfather John T. Hoover owned slaves in 1725 and was using black slave women as bed-warmers. So, Ivery and his daughter Mozilla decided they were going to take this matter into their own hands, and they weren't going to keep the family decade-old secrets any longer. They felt especially since slavery was over, and it shouldn't matter. Also, we all knew that J. Edgar was Uncle Ivery's biological son and Mozilla's half-brother. So, all our lives were in danger.

Well, that was not going to work out well for J. Edgar Hoover, so he threatened to harm them both if they broke the family code and told the secret of his ethnicity to the world."

When Big Daddy finished telling Millie that story, she was fearful, but she wanted to know more about what happened to Uncle Ivery, and his daughter Mozilla although Millie understood and decided to keep the secret? It was clear J. Edgar Hoover wasn't happy with them both, and a few months later the family got a big bombshell!

Millie's mother was listening to her father tell his granddaughter the family history because she knew that Millie wasn't going to stop until she had heard it all. So, her mother came out on the porch and joined Big Daddy in telling the story to Millie, she said,

"I wasn't born yet, but this story was told at every family reunion as I was growing up. There were rumors all through the family at that time about two murders. They were both found dead but at different times. It was reported to us that Uncle Ivery was trying to reason with J. Edgar as a father would his son, but again, J. Edgar wasn't ready to believe it was safe for him to be black, so they had a falling out. Soon after their argument on November 18, 1917, just six days before Uncle Ivery's fifty-eighth birthday, he was found dead. It was said that this was no surprise to the family members, but they knew he was murdered. Then everyone was afraid to do or say anything, so they decided to go on and have his funeral and keep silent. Although I wasn't born yet, the rumors have been passed down through generations. We have to keep his secret, or we would die like Uncle Ivery. I heard how sad it was at his funeral."

Millie listened intensely to her mother's storytelling, but although she was fearful, she wanted to know it all, so her mother continued,

"I was told that FBI agents were attending, and everyone tried to tell Mozilla not to speak about J. Edgar being Uncle Ivery's son and her half-brother at the funeral. She told the family that she was going to the newspapers to tell the entire story about her father's outside illegitimate-son that was working in the government, who had his own father murdered. It was said that J. Edgar didn't attend the funeral, but I'm sure the FBI agents reported back to J. Edgar about Mozilla's outburst and her threats to go to the newspaper. In the news, J. Edgar had just gotten his law degree, and during the time of Uncle Ivery's funeral he passed the bar exam hoping to get a promotion on his job."

"In 1917 J. Edgar Hoover was working for the Library of Congress, he took night classes at George Washington University Law School, and had just earned his LLB (bachelor of laws) and LLM (master of laws) degrees, during the death of Ivery Hoover. The United States had just entered World War I during that same time."

(https://www.history.com/topics/us-government/j-edgar-hoover)

Millie's mother had a relationship with a daughter of Mozilla's; she called her "Kane." They both told Millie the rumors they remembered about J. Edgar not attending Ivery's funeral. However, he had eyes and ears spying for him and was having Mozilla watched. The family knew it wasn't smart of her talking about going to the newspaper. They tried to keep her quiet for the sake of her five young children, and "Kane" was one of them. They told her that it was bad timing to go to the newspaper since her father was just found dead, which kept her quiet for a few months.

In 1927 Mozilla was 31 years old when they found her dead, leaving five children and a husband. Again, everyone in the family knew what had happened and was afraid to say anything; they just had her funeral and buried her quietly. There was no death certificate to be found for Mozilla, nor any police report acknowledging her death. It was like she vanished! Now, that's why the entire family has sworn to keep this secret.

As Millie's Mother continued to tell her the story about the two murders in the family, Millie was trying to figure out the reason why the secrets had to remain within the family after so many years. However, she found it to be more and more fearful in her young heart. Big Daddy, as well as her mother, didn't pull any punches in adamantly and repeatedly cautioning her as well as, the rest of the family. They made it crystal clear that immediate harm would come to members of the family if the secret of the biological father of J. Edgar were talked about even to friends, unveiled in writing, or if it fell into the wrong hands it could be immediate death to the family as long as J. Edgar Hoover was alive.

The public believes one thing, but our family members knew the truth. Millie soon realized it was imperative that she kept quiet for the protection of her family. She decided to lock those stories and J. Edgar Hoover secret way down into her unconscious mind. Millie never spoke of it to Big Daddy or anyone else in her family during her childhood.

When Millie left her grandfather's house that day, she was so frightened and couldn't get those stories that were family secrets out of her head about the two murders. When those memories came into her mind from time to time of family members being murdered because they were planning to tell that secret, it was terrifying.

She remembered when they all returned to their apartment in the projects after leaving Big Daddy's house, she jumped out of the car, ran into the bedroom that the girls shared so she could be along to pray before the other sisters came into the bedroom. She wanted to pray to God to help her keep those secret deep inside her soul for her entire family's safety. She asked God for protection in helping her keep the secret with Big Daddy.

During her life going forward as a child, things were so different for her after that day. She didn't want to go to any more family reunions but when she did attend she closed her mind when they started the storytelling about their ancestors.

It wasn't until she was all grown up with a family of her own when the nightmares started to come that would frighten her out of her sleep night after night. As the years went past and Millie grew into womanhood, memories soon began to drift into her dreams trying to surface through those nightmares. The time that she spent with her Big Daddy and mother was so special. Nevertheless, she didn't realize the impact that time would have on her as an adult.

The knowledge of her roots is something that she will keep with her forever and enjoy sharing it with family. She encouraged others to start making time for the elders in their family before it's too late.

The history of many family roots back in time was stored in the mind of the elders who lived before you. When Millie was a child, she felt it was a joy for her to be in the company of the elders. She loved listening to them tell her stories about their ancestors. Although, some family stories were secrets and were frightening. Sometimes when she was listening to the elders in her family's storytelling, she could visualize them in her mind and felt as though she shared a glimpse into their past watching them farming, planting, weeding, taking care of the animals, and even working in the cotton fields. Millie also had a chance to pick cotton in the cotton fields as a child, and she said it was hard work. She learned so much from Big Daddy about how life was in the 1800s. He told her stories about why they had so many children that were born at home, and many of other family members children died before they were five years old due to dysentery, typhoid, scarlet fever or measles.

Millie started to think in her mind,

"Big Daddy was blessed with all sixteen of his children that lived to become good adults." I think Millie's mother told her they lost one child, and it was a twin, one lived, and the other one died.

Now all grown up, Millie started to reminisce of the oral history stories that were told to her by the elders, family reunions and sitting under Big Daddy's legs. Many times before he said to her that the traditional storytelling went all the way back to Africa where a family member would tell the others the facts of our beginnings. Millie's mother, Alberta Allen, and her grandfather, Clarence Allen ("Big Daddy") were the storytellers and her heroes because they took the time to tell her about their family history.

"Now, Millie is the storyteller. "

Big Daddy and her mother continued to tell the stories about three very strong women that started their family on Mr. Allen's plantation. Millie understood that the first woman was taken from West Africa at 16 years old; her name was Sarah, at first Millie didn't know her name, so she referred to her as just 'Grandma Elizabeth's Mother,' who was impregnated with Elizabeth by her slave owner, whom Millie soon found out to be a man named Mr. Allen. A man not talked about during the storytelling during the reunions. Millie wanted to know more about him, and nobody said who he was, other than he owned slaves.

As Big Daddy finished the story, Millie thought,

"This family's oral history is starting to sound like a shocking revelation and unbelievable."

Millie now all grown up and even more addicted to researching her family's history to find the entire story in census records and the documents with dates of birth, death and marriage records in the archives to see how Emily lived and had her babies. She needed proof!

Chapter 3

THE JOURNEY

The time had come for Millie to make that journey back home to her roots. She needed to decide as to opening up this can of worms now that J. Edgar Hoover was no longer a threat. She chose for this research to be completed using one of the world's extensive genealogical libraries, which she found was in Salt Lake City, UT. There would be the census records, birth record, marriage recordings, and you could discover in records who were slave owners in Mississippi that are kept safe in the many Historical Libraries.

Millie had to know the truth and found this work to be the most freeing experience in her life. She said that it felt like she was walking with her ancestors to open this door for the truth to set them free so they could to rest in peace. Millie needed to let go of this secret so she could move forward as well. The greatest experience was Millie's trip back home to Mississippi and New Orleans with her Mother, father, newfound Hoover white-cousins Kristy, and her family. Clayton A. Hoover was the great-grandfather of Kristy and J. Edgar Hoover claimed his side of the Hoover family. This trip was important to both sides of the family. They were all in awe over being on the grounds in Mississippi where their ancestors walked, lived, and died.

Millie had all the information about how the Allen's and the Hoover's were connected. It helped find J. Edgar Hoover's biological father's resting place marked right on the Hoover's Plantation. He was buried with the "White Hoovers" and only a few feet from his grandfather the slave owner, Christian Hoover who was born in 1796. Ivery was given the Hoover name because he was born on November 24, the same day as his grandfather Christian Hoover. Our genealogist said this was a significant find, it was the key to the connection with J. Edgar Hoover.

Millie's desire now was to share this with people all over the world about this journey with her white cousin's taking pictures of their remarkable, fantastic, and also scary sometimes because it was painful venturing into finding her roots, then to learn of the three women as bed-warmers for the slave owners. There are photos and documents of the research shown in the photo album section of this book.

Millie begins with the lectures informing people of how her journey helped her find the documents and census records that would connect the two families, "The Allen's and Hoover's," which prompted many questions. Here are a few of the questions from the events and Millie below answered the questions:

(Q) What does it mean to you personally to go on this journey?

Millie's answer: "Visiting my old homestead in Mississippi has always been full of memories, but this time I wasn't just going on a trip to visit family or to have a vacation, and it turned out to be much more than that for me. I was on a journey to find myself and speak to my ancestors.

My parents accompanied me on this trip, which was great because now my mother was the storyteller of it all. I knew this journey was going to involve traveling long distances and was going to be often dangerous or difficult circumstances. Not because I was going to be crossing deserts, but because I was inquiring into the lives of other people who may not want to know this part of their history or even know me. I knew my visit would be neither brief nor swift or even an ordinary journey.

This journey would flow through many states in the United States of America. I would meet some of the most beautiful and angry people of all races. However, the most important thing to me coming out of this work would be that my ancestors would rest in peace finally, and I would be free. I was fortunate because this journey wasn't taken with me alone, but with family and Historical Genealogist to help me with details within the documents. We were a team of beautiful people who traveled together on this soul-searching experience. We went by train, car, limousine, and airplanes.

The group of us walked through graveyards, many cities, old historical homes, museums, and also libraries. Then ventured through the thick woods trying to find the place where my Big Daddy's house stood before it burned down and where he raised those sixteen children; of which, one was my mother, Alberta Allen-McGhee.

This was a spiritual journey for me; the stories I was told as a child stayed with me until I was all grown up. However, there was something I really was puzzled about concerning the Allen's and Hoover's.

"How did Sarah, Elizabeth, and Emily get the surname Allen?" They got it from their slave owner.

Since Elizabeth and Emily had babies by Hoover men. Then just before the second printing of this book, I found out the answer to that question. You will read about that later in the book. I felt my ancestors with me in the process of comprehending how they had to live during slavery while researching my roots. I felt I was getting an education, and through the enlightenment for me into their once existence on earth was a unique experience. It was an individual breakthrough for me to attain reconciliation and edification in finding my spirit within my ancestors into my roots."

(Q) Why was it important to find your soul in this process?

Millie's answer: "My belief is that a person's contribution to society is important to his or her legacy left to inspire generations to come. Also, the knowledge and experiences a person has is a vital role in determining his or her position in their life. I felt it was important to me to make sure that the connections to the Allen family and the Hoover's were accurate to share with generations to come.

I think knowing your roots and the people that you are related to can be healthy. Perhaps you would need a transplant or blood infusion, and finding the correct or same blood type could be vital to your healing,

When I started this journey, I faced all kinds of roadblocks, evil spirits trying to stop me, but I never gave up. I believe I had the sense of my ancestors intervening on my behalf against the evil spirits. In my heart, I know my ancestors wanted this story of truth to be acknowledged.

Due to my current successes in life, I'm always being asked, "If you had to do this work all over again what would you do differently?" Well, I believe the real question is, "Was all that pain and suffering worth it?" My answer is YES to both questions. As I was enduring the pain and suffering, I almost wanted to just quit, but my ancestors wouldn't let me. Now that this work has finished, I'm happy I didn't quit. I wouldn't have wanted this any other way."

(Q) How did you feel when the white Hoover family reached out to you?

Millie's answer: "It was surreal. My first glance into Kristy L. Hoover-Sullivan's face, I saw kindness. We spent the entire day together; we were family from the beginning.

(I've included pictures of our trip together during research in the photo album in this book). I took Kristy and her daughter to meet my mother before she died. Kristy took one look at mother and said, "It's like looking in a mirror."

Kristy was surprised to find her great-grandfather Clayton A Hoover's named in Millie's research. She then said; "The whole idea of our strand of Hoovers with history in Washington, DC having anything to do with slaves was a difficult concept to swallow. We were naturally skeptical and as far from slavery as we could get."

Millie replied to her; "As I said before, it is not our ancestor's deeds that define us; it's our deeds that mark our legacy."

(Q) What do you feel today about your relationship with the White Hoovers?

Millie's answer: "I felt our ancestor's spirit being pleased with us. We will always love them and call them family. It was a pleasure having her and her daughter Haley with us on the trip to Mississippi, to walk on land where I was born and raised."

Kristy said, "Whether or not DNA proves our connection, Millie and I are here for the same purpose. I believe that healing our planet starts with healing ourselves. We agreed to want children to live in a world where the content of their character is more important than the color of their skin." Millie replied, "I am grateful."

(Q) What kind of obstacles did you come across during the 21 years?

Millie's answer: "What are the challenges in life? In our personal lives on a worldwide scale, we will face challenges that will test our emotions on a daily bases. We face accidents, fires, injury, illness, unemployment, grief, divorce, death, and even evil attacks trying to stop a new undertaking with an unforeseen future like this one you are reading. I started this research 21 years ago, and it has been one thing after another trying to stop this work from becoming a reality. I was in an accident that caused me seven years to get back on my feet, another car accident in 2017, and I almost gave up. My faith kept me going, and I never looked back. The spirit of God was leading me to my ancestors who guided and protected me through the hands of God."

(Q) Did you feel this was worth it?

Millie's answer: "When it was all said and done, and after looking back at how far I've come, my faith is even stronger in the power of God. I feel that no matter what anyone thinks or says, in my heart I know without a shadow of a doubt, this work was worth everything that came my way and into my life. This book was worth all the heartaches, pain, and suffering. I feel that way because I am free from hiding all those secrets for over 61 years now. My prayer is that maybe others with this burden will take up the cross and become free too, by following the spirit of God."

Now, Millie will take you on a journey through finding the truth in the reviewing of the facts about the documents she recovered in the archives, libraries, and her research starting with chapter 4.

Chapter 4

ORAL VS. DOCUMENTED

Oral History was essential for Millie to learn about their start in life and about the three slave women who gave them life. It was important to her especially since slaves were not allowed to learn how to read or write during slavery. Since Millie didn't learn how to read until she was 47-years-old. During her research, they discovered documents revealing how the Hoover and Allen families were connected base on the oral history and the census records.

Now, at this point you the reader, should watch for the main characters of men listed below as the story of the ten-year-old Millie's account of the oral tale unfolds. Now, 71-year-old Millie with the spirit of her ancestors in her mind will be unveiling the stories following the census, and archives records. Now, as you go forward below are the names of the men family members that are key characters to follow:

➢ Christian Hoover born in 1796

➢ Mr. Allen born in 1794

➢ William Hoover born in 1804

- ➢ Jeff McComb

- ➢ William Hoover born in 1832

- ➢ Christian "Kit" Hoover born 1840

- ➢ Ivy/Ivery Hoover born 1859

- ➢ William Hoover born in 1870

- ➢ Clarence Allen born in 1893

- ➢ J. Edgar Hoover born in 1895

Then the list of women characters in Millie's family that are key to this shocking truth and lies saga of decade-old family stories regarding the treatment of white women and slave women:

- ➢ Sarah Allen, the 16-year-old (black) West African.

- ➢ Mary Neyland Hoover (white) Married Christian in 1823.

- ➢ Martha Leticia Jane Thompson Hoover (white)

- ➢ Elizabeth Allen Hoover born about 1805 a slave

- ➢ Arie Hoover (black) was married to Ivery Hoover

- ➢ Emily Allen born about 1838 a slave

- ➢ Susannah Sophia Holbrook (white) about 1848,

J. Edgar Hoover thought his secret would never come to light, but a ten-year-old girl heard it all and kept this priceless history hidden inside her mind for over 70 years now; bottled up deep down inside her soul. Here are more recounts of that little girl.

Let's start with her story about the sixteen-year-old slave girl Sarah, who was brought out of West Africa that was sold to Mr. Allen, with no first name that Millie had found in research. He was a Mississippi slave owner who owned slaves on his plantation. The 16-year-old slave girl Sarah was brought out of West Africa and soon made a slave on the Plantation in Mississippi owned by Mr. Allen. Sarah became his slave bed-warmer. He soon impregnated Sarah and had a girl they named Elizabeth Allen. The child was given the slave owner's surname. The women of the slave owners were called bed-warmers, the owners had sex with them and they were married men. The slave women had children for them. In this case, the child's last name should have been 'Allen," However, the way Millie's Big Daddy got his last name was different. Elizabeth was later impregnated by Mr. Allen her father and gave birth to another girl they named Emily Allen, and you will learn more about her later in the book.

Millie was excited to find an Allen cousin who had researched her family roots on the Allen side of the family and discovered that Millie was related to her, and that they were cousins. The information she found help Millie learn how her Big Daddy got the Allen surname instead of the surname of his grandfather, William Hoover (1832). We will get to that later in the book.

Millie understood that black families' history was never put into records/documented in the census records during slavery. So, all she had was the oral tales/story to depend on in her family's case, which was handed down stories at family reunions or storytelling by the elders to the family member that was interested like Millie. Oral history to Millie was a collection of information given to her from the elders, to keep the family traditional history preserved for future generations.

Since Millie was chosen to keep the family history alive, she wanted to find out if any of the words of mouth stories might have been written in any documents in the census. So, she joined the best African American historical groups and with the world's most extensive genealogical library personnel in Salt Lake City, UT. They assisted her in the journey. It's good to learn that this library has experienced guides and genealogists that help with family research.

Millie discovers a collection of records at the library in Salt Lake City, UT. She got many of the census records that matched oral history. The truth about her family and the connection between the Hoover families and Allen was discovered in the census record and vital record.

She started in 1997, and by 2000 she had found documents that were connecting her to the oral history. It was exciting; she had a lot of the papers, census records, birth, and death certificates. However, Millie didn't know how to arrange what she had found within the narrative in chronological order to align with the oral family history to be able to see the story.

So, Millie researched how to use oral history and documented history to find a match. She noticed on the

Internet organizations that had genealogy historians who understood how to find and connect the records to oral history. Millie joined the Afro-American Historical and Genealogical Society (AAHGS). She was pleased to obtain two of the best Genealogist/Historians assisting her in connecting the documents and census records research that she found. They helped her match the oral family history to the documents.

Millie worked with the late great Genealogist and Historians, Lucius Bowser, and Julian Burke who were the honored members of AAHGS, for over ten years, whom Millie have stated she misses dearly.

Millie did her DNA to find out what part of Africa did her bloodline originate. She found out that she came from West Africa, which was "The Guinea-Bissau Tribe." Millie believed that the 16-year-old slave girl Sarah came out of West Africa also, and was from the, "Guinea-Bissea Tribe."

Millie thought that was the key. Why? Millie found out from her research that the "Guinea-Bissea Tribe," had many mulatto people living on the land in 1997. Then, she remembered what her mother asked Big Daddy when she was a child,

"Daddy, why do Grandma Emily look like a white lady? I thought Africans were dark skin people."

Her mother asked that question when she was a child, and now Millie had the answer. Grandma Emily was a mulatto slave offspring of the white men that went over to

West Africa and impregnated the women on the land. Then left their offspring in the belly of the African women. They fathered these half white babies and just left, many of them didn't even know that they had fathered a child, which was why Millie thought this book was even more profound than what was being told about J. Edgar Hoover's lies, secrets, and deceit as being part of her family.

Millie said,

"This is why I felt the Mulatto-women of this tribe came from the White Men who went over to West Africa and sexually abused, used them as what was called bed-warming, impregnated them, and they fathered children that they left behind. *(Maybe didn't even know)* They had their fun with the women while they were looking for strong slaves to work their land, and left their bed-warmers with half white babies to raise in a poor country. Those babies grew up, then they became adults. Then this vicious cycle would start over again, "Slave Trade, and sexual abuse/bed-warmer upon those half-white children of the white men."

They were called, "Mulatto."

In Millie's family, the oral storytellers were Big Daddy, her mother Alberta, her mother's Sister Lillian, and now Millie.

We begin with the slave owner, Christian Hoover. He was the beginning of it all in Big Daddy's family. He fathered with Mary Hoover Big Daddy's father's-father, who was named William Hoover (1832). Millie followed that sixteen your old slave girl Sarah out of West Africa to America she belong to Mr. Allen's place. Millie felt she needed to remember that because it was connected to her birth, because without her Big Daddy, Millie may not have been born.

This is the story about Sarah; a slave owner Mr. Allen owned her, he had a plantation in Pike County, Mississippi. When he purchased Sarah she was only 16-years-old. She thought he hired her to be a maid in his home in American to help her family. Now, we all know that wasn't the case. Sarah was given the surname of Allen, and impregnated by Mr. Allen as soon as she was on his plantation in America. The 16-years-old Sarah child was called Elizabeth Allen, and as soon as she was of child bearing age Mr. Allen impregnated his own daughter. She bore a girl child also, and named her Emily Allen.

Now, this is how they got to the Hoover plantation. When Emily was very young her mother Elizabeth Allen met William Hoover born in 1805 a single man, and they started an affair. He impregnated her with her second child and they had a son, which they named John T. Hoover. Christian Hoover 1796 and William Hoover 1805 were brothers, so the oral story stated.

William wanted to marry Elizabeth Allen the slave girl, and made arrangement for Emily Allen to be bought by Christian Hoover to live on the Hoover land.

The following research will display a look into the recorded documents found with the Hoovers dates of birth, death and the names of the family member. We will also outline how the children were born within the white family and the children born with the slave women. The story begins with Christian Hoover born in 1796, his two sons William Hoover born in 1832, and Christian "Kit" Hoover born in 1840. Then they would find themselves intertwined with the slave "Mulatto" women Emily Allen. It would be so twisted that it was no way of hiding the truth. Millie found family records grouping the family tree of Hoovers and Allen's as one family.

Christian Hoover that was born in 1796, in South Carolina, and he died in 1868. He was also a wealthy cotton plantation owner in Pike County, Mississippi. He was a Minister, a state Legislator, and owner of over one hundred slaves. Millie's great-great-grandmother Emily Allen was part of his collection, and she was family.

Elizabeth had to leave Emily on the plantation with her in-laws, so she thought. The negotiation was set up between family member William Hoover who was born in 1804, and his brother Christian Hoover born in 1796.

It was said through out the family that William Hoover 1804, took one look at Elizabeth and wanted her for his wife, and after the birth of their son John T. Hoover, he took her to the Maryland/DC area, they married, and she passed for white her entire life.

Although, Emily was Elizabeth's daughter, William Hoover wasn't her father, old man Mr. Allen was Emily's father and grandfather it was, "Incest!" Mr. Allen sold

Emily to Christian without any hesitation. Millie discovered the document showing her in family records passing for white.

The records showed Christian Hoover married Mary Neyland on April 8, 1823, and they had twelve children before her death on February 3, 1858. She was only fifty-one years old when she died, which was very young. Mary left him with young children. She knew about him going into the slave quarters and having sexual encounters with the slave girls. Most of his children by Mary Neyland died young; before the age of thirty-one. Only two of them shown in the records lived past fifty.

Millie's Big Daddy's grandfather was one of them, William Hoover born in 1832; he fathered six of Emily's children.

See Chart of:

Christian Hoover and Mary N. Hoover's list of children on the next page.

Christian's wife Mary Neyland died leaving him with three children under nineteen years of age. It was sad that two of their children died before she did. *(Millie thought, it must have been tough losing those children at such an early age.)*

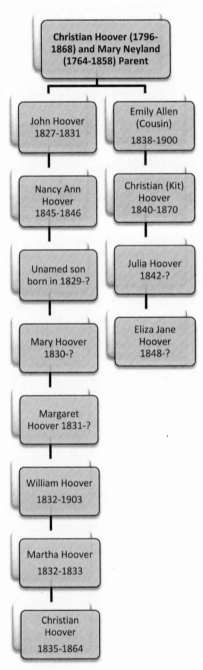

His first wife Mary died February 3, 1858; it was only one year and one month after the death of Mary that he married Susannah. Christian was then sixty-three years old, and Susannah was forty-one.

The researchers discerned in the documents that Christian remarried soon after the death of his wife of thirty-five years. It appeared that he was having an affair with his second wife before the death of his first wife because they had children together before Mary's death. The adulterous Susannah's children were listed in the census during the time Mary was alive, and still having children with her husband. *He married Susannah Sophia Holbrook on March 26, 1859, in Louisiana in the New Orleans Parish.* Now keep in mind he was having children by Susannah before his wife Mary died. Mary died in 1958.

See the chart listing the children of Christian Hoover and *Susannah Sophia Holbrook* on the next page...

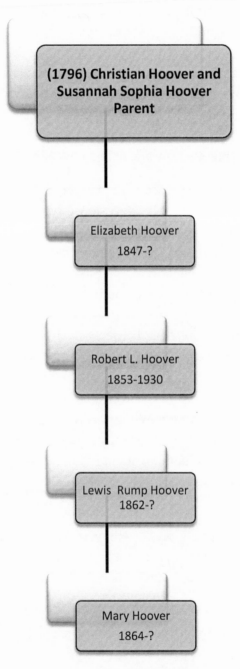

(1796) Christian Hoover and Susannah Sophia Hoover Parent

Elizabeth Hoover
1847-?

Robert L. Hoover
1853-1930

Lewis Rump Hoover
1862-?

Mary Hoover
1864-?

After Mary's birth, six years later, her father died at the age of seventy-two. Susannah was only forty-six; still a young woman. When Christian passed away, he left his young wife with three young children, but he left her in good care. His son William Hoover born 1832, who was my Big Daddy's grandfather, he was thirty-six years old when he inherited the slaves from his father and now was left to look after his stepmother Susannah and three siblings.

Christian Hoover who was born in 1796 fathered nineteen (16) children between those two women. He was an adulterous. This man was a renowned Mississippi Judge, a State Legislator, a State Senator, and a Minister for the county. He had relatives as well as business acquaintances in Washington, D.C., and owned over 100 slaves.

(Millie thought, "Powerful men had their way with women, no matter the race, as far back as the 1700s.")

When Christian Hoover died, he left his legacy and his business to his son William Hoover. Millie was happy to find out all about Christian through research because it helped her find a lot more about her oral history storytelling given to her.

Now, that William Hoover (1832) has inherited the slave, Emily. She's on the Hoover plantation and William Hoover a married man learned from his father "Christian Hoover," of being an adulterous.

You will notice how much he loved and respected his father Christian Hoover also a married man, and how he treated his wife and his slaves. William Hoover was very proud of his father and he showed it by naming his firstborn after the old man.

A son following in his father's footsteps, and not the footsteps of God!

Chapter 5

EMILY AND MARTHA

Millie noticed many sons named William. At this point, she realized the need to use birth dates when referring to them to identify who's who. In her family, there were many men with the name William Hoover' they were born in these years: 1804, 1832, 1855, 1863, and 1870. So identifying anyone in the family named William Hoover or William Allen you needed to know the birth year.

William, Christian, John, or Joseph Hoover you needed to use the year of their birth to know who's who. This was also true to the Allen family men and women.

The William Hoover, who was born in 1832, son of Senator Christian Hoover, was married to Martha Leticia Jane Thompson. They married on July 27, 1852, and had nine children; and he had six children with Emily Allen his slave girl/cousin during the same time of having children with his wife Martha. William had a pattern that was passed down through generations of using slave women as bed-warmers. It held to be true when the first child was born with William 1832 and Martha as the mother, and he soon got into bed with Emily his slave/cousin-in-law in this pattern. The first child with Martha was born 1853; they named him Christian R. Hoover, after his father. See the Chart on the next page to continue his pattern.

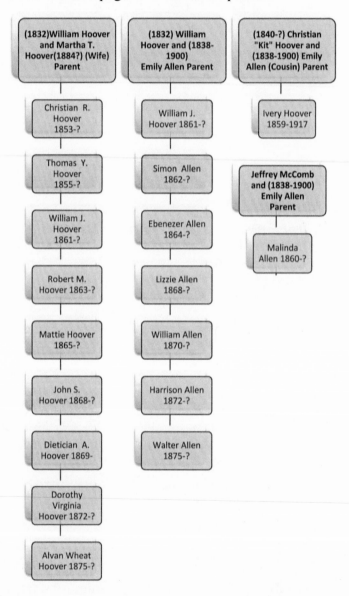

(1832)William Hoover and Martha T. Hoover(1884?) (Wife) Parent	(1832) William Hoover and (1838-1900) Emily Allen Parent	(1840-?) Christian "Kit" Hoover and (1838-1900) Emily Allen (Cousin) Parent
Christian R. Hoover 1853-?	William J. Hoover 1861-?	Ivery Hoover 1859-1917
Thomas Y. Hoover 1855-?	Simon Allen 1862-?	Jeffrey McComb and (1838-1900) Emily Allen Parent
William J. Hoover 1861-?	Ebenezer Allen 1864-?	Malinda Allen 1860-?
Robert M. Hoover 1863-?	Lizzie Allen 1868-?	
Mattie Hoover 1865-?	William Allen 1870-?	
John S. Hoover 1868-?	Harrison Allen 1872-?	
Dietician A. Hoover 1869-	Walter Allen 1875-?	
Dorothy Virginia Hoover 1872-?		
Alvan Wheat Hoover 1875-?		

William Hoover 1832 had fathered sixteen of the seventeen children born at this point. His brother Christian 'Kit' Hoover had fathered Ivery Hoover with Emily, who was his cousin. William allowed a friend Jeff McComb to get in bed with Emily and he fathered Emily's daughter Malinda Allen she still carried her mother's surname.

Millie wondered if those ladies were aware of each other's pregnancies. Millie said, "In my heart, I will believe they were aware."

Back in those days, men did whatever they wanted to do, and their wives were afraid to say anything. Some of the white women were treated like slaves as well because if they said anything, their husband would abuse them. Emily, the slave, lived on the plantation, and Martha lived in the main house with William Hoover, her husband. In the census group records, Emily was listed as William's wife, but he was still married to Martha and having children by them both.

Emily had seven children that carried her surname, which was, Allen, and one child that carried the Hoover, surname. The child was Ivery Hoover, fathered by Christian 'Kit' Hoover. Then Emily had all of her other children by William Hoover born 1832.

Millie asked her mother and Big Daddy why Ivery Hoover got to carry the surname Hoover. She was told he looked white with blue eyes, and skin as white as snow.

Millie didn't believe that was the only reason, and later when she discovered his gravestone right on the Hoover plantation alongside the white family. She noticed the birth dates of Ivery Hoover born November 24, 1859, alongside Christian Hoover born November 24, 1796. Millie knew she had the real correct answer, Ivy was born on the head master's birthday, and they felt it was a sign. Millie was sure they meant for him to pass for white, but he didn't because he wanted two pretty slave women, Anna, and Arie.

Now we will go through more of the documented records of how it played out in Millie's family. Emily is the critical person to Ivery, J. Edgar, and Clarence, who is Millie's grandfather "Big Daddy."

Millie noticed Elizabeth Allen, who married to William Hoover had impregnated her before they left the plantation headed to the Maryland/DC area. They had a son that they named John T. Hoover.

William Hoover, who was born in 1832, fathered six of Emily's children. He was her cousin-in-law and the slave owner.

Then another child with Emily was fathered by Christian's "Kit," and this child was given the Hoover surname. That child was named, Ivery Hoover. William and Christian "kit" was Emily's cousin-in-law.

Millie has discovered Ivery Hoover's death record and now knows that he was J. Edgar Hoover's biological father, as the oral history stated. He was born November 24,

1859, and died November 18, 1917, just six days before his 58th birthday. Death certificate states no doctor, no obituary, nothing in the newspaper, and no cause of death on death record. "It was said that his son, J. Edgar Hoover ordered his death, and he had been murdered to hide the truth, of the family oral history." J. Edgar Hoover was 22 years old and already working for the FBI when Ivery Hoover was murdered.

Millie said, "In my mind, I thought that these women cared a lot about each other. I believed that William loved Emily because they stayed together until death.

Information was found in the 1900 census showing that Martha finally divorced William and moved to Texas, where she died at the age of eighty-two on September 18, 1916. William died before her on January 14, 1903, at the age of seventy-one. The records showed Emily Allen died about 1913, at the age of seventy-five.

(Millie was impressed with how long Martha and Emily lived after having so many babies, so close together, and at the same time Millie was angry because she saw it as sexual abuse. They had a baby every year for about eight years.)

There is so much more to this story, and now we are going into the census records. How do Millie and J. Edgar Hoover's life coincide? Emily Allen was J. Edger Hoover's grandmother and Millie's great-great-grandmother.

When Millie lived in Mississippi, and Big Daddy gave her the story at the age of ten, it was then when their lives started to burn into one unit of fear. J. Edgar's fear was different from Millie's fear, but yet it was fear all the same.

Mille remembers a day while writing down the story her Big Daddy and mother had told her and now she was all grown up in California. She saw J. Edgar's spirit come into her home and tried to frightened her, and Millie said all at the same time her ancestors came into her spirit to assure her that J. Edgar Hoover couldn't harm her now.

Millie said, "My ancestors were with me all through this journey!"

Chapter 6

MILLIE AND J. EDGAR

As a child, Millie assumed that some of her family knew about J. Edgar's relationship and connection to their family but they all dared to speak of it. She recalls occasions when members of the family would flip on the television and jimmying the long adjustable rabbit ears to get a clear picture when Hoover appeared on the small black/white screen. It was during the time of Martin Luther King Jr. Millie said she would get angry when she saw J. Edgar Hoover speak unkind words about Martin Luther King because there was something about Hoover Millie didn't like, but couldn't remember at that time in the 1960s what had her troubled. She did feel Mr. Hoover had secrets. She did, but she was suppressing the thoughts of it. In the Black community where she lived, they believed that Hoover had something to do with the death of Dr. King.

Today that Mississippi poor government project little girl is different. Now she's called, Dr. Millie McGhee-Morris by many business owners, with her credentials like you, wouldn't believe; her being an author, a publisher, a mentor, an inspirational speaker, an educator, a multi-entrepreneurial, and philanthropist. However, and nobody knew she was suffering in silence trying to hide the dark secrets that she carried inside that were haunting her for decades.

Millie was born during the baby boomer area and raised in the government projects in a small plantation town called, McComb, Mississippi. She was the third child of ten born to Reverend William Allen and Alberta McGhee. As early as Millie could remember she demonstrated a great desire for leadership by helping the younger children that lived in her neighborhood through the work in her father's ministry. She has a slogan, which Millie wanted it to be her philosophy and it was, *"Be inspiring, and remember you can do anything you set your mind to do; if you truly believe in yourself."*

Millie cultivated her entrepreneurship businesses by serving as a spokesperson for her father on a radio program spiritual ministry every Sunday morning when she was a young teen. Thankfully this work allowed her to hone in on her communication skills and positioned herself to become a radio host at the age of sixteen thus laying the foundation toward shaping a future path.

In 1965 after high school she had high hopes of attending college. Unfortunately, those plans were derailed, due to her inadequacies in academic skills. When she was applying to colleges, Millie discovered her problems with her substandard education and being nearly illiterate. Millie found a way to improve her education to complete what she wanted to become, which was a published author.

Millie was responsible for moving her parents and young sibling out of the McComb city government project in 1967, to California even with the substandard education. She knew how to make friends and ask for help.

In 1984, Millie's dear friend Cynthia Stewart, who was a teacher, as well as a fellow advocate of Millie's ideas regarding starting a youth program in California. They met in California; this teacher worked very hard to re-educate Millie. Subsequently, Millie brought her beliefs and dreams to fruition and established "The Young Talented Achievers Educational Pageant" (YTAEP) in 1984, due to the help of Cynthia Stewart.

The program was founded based on the premise of providing a platform for struggling students in Middle School inspired by Millie's personal-childhood challenges.

It was a program that was designed to provide students with encouragement and resources that helped aid them throughout their academic performance. Millie didn't learn how to read until the age of 43, and she developed into a fierce advocate for literacy education for adolescents, adults, and seniors.

Millie's first four marriages didn't last, due to her being battered by her husbands and her inadequacies, but Millie prayed and began educating herself. Millie soon realized if she was to get what was essential in her life, she had to improve her education, and she did. In 1990 she met and married the love of her life, Dr. Leslie Morris.

In 1997, Millie became interested in finding her roots. This assertion arose after a Niece called a family meeting to explain what she called, "A family curse due to many sexual encounters with family members. Millie wasn't sure of how much she may find in researching their family roots in writing as to documents. However, she was now motivated.

Millie, all grown up now. After the first four years of research, she noticed what was labeled a generational curse. She based that on sexual encounters with the women in her family back in the days of slavery, it was prevalent. The slave owners were having sex with their children born of their "slave-bed-warmer." There are many young people today have never heard the phrase, "Bed-warmer" which was a slave woman that is sexually abused by the slave owner. Now, what would it be called today with fathers, brothers, and cousins getting into bed with the women in the family? Millie wondered, but she called it "Incest Bed-Raping."

While working on the research for her family roots, Millie found the connection to J. Edgar Hoover's family, and this information opened her mind to the memory that had been buried into her mind when she was a child. Since the nightmares pieces of her memory were coming back, she felt a need to ask her mother this question,

"Mom, can you tell me if we are directly related to the FBI director J. Edgar Hoover?"

Her mother answered, "Yes."

This led Millie straight to the library. She found a book in the library that was written by Curt Gentry entitled, "J. Edgar Hoover: The Man and the Secrets," an 800-page book and she checked it out to read.

Later when she walked into her mother's home with the book in her hand, and her mother saw the picture of J. Edgar Hoover placed directly on the front of the book and Millie's mother said,

"Oh my! Granddad! Where did you find a book with my granddad on the cover?"

Millie replied to her mother, "Mom no, this is not your granddad! This is J. Edgar Hoover."

Millie asked more questions.

"Mom, please tell me more about the Hoover family connection to our family?"

"Well, it was a family secret that Uncle Ivery and J. Edgar Hoover's mother were lovers and J. Edgar Hoover was their bastard child," replied her mother.

The answer to that question inspired Millie to move forward and find the connection in documents. She knew that Oral History wasn't accepted as an authentic truth or respected. She also knew this work was not going to be easy, with finding oral history in documents. It was clear to her traveling to Salt Lake City, UT to review the census records was something that was needed. Millie decided to travel to the library in Salt Lake City, UT and noticed while reviewing the records that the census keeper's on occasions misspelled individuals' information such as, their name and date of birth could have been incorrect back in the day. The individuals would spell their name differently on other documents, which could take you off track. It didn't matter, because Millie was on this journey to find the real authentic documents regarding Ivy or Ivery and Anna or Annie in the census records.

She found information about John Edgar Hoover's roots; he was born in 1895 in Washington, DC. He was a student at George Washington University taking classes at night to get his degree. J. Edgar worked at the Library of Congress as a clerk during the day.

J. Edgar graduated in 1917, and he was accepted to the bar in Washington, DC and the Justice Department at the age of 22-years young. During Millie's research into his life, she noticed other discrepancies, which reminded her of what Big Daddy said about finding his birth record,

"You won't find it, because he will erase it."

J. Edgar Hoover seemingly learned all his bad habits out of fear trying to cover-up his roots. He was the manager of the General Intelligence Division in the bureau where he gathered evidence on radical groups, and he was good at his job. Strangely, many observers and even experts felt there's not a great deal else of consequence to learn about J. Edgar Hoover that hasn't been said or done over the years and all the skeletons were out of his closet.

Millie didn't agree, saying,

"I don't think so!"

Millie could say with confidence this time that she has shocking revelations and the evidence to prove it! She has her oral history, 21-years of documents, census records and family video recording of her mother and father, to show the doubters. Those who say there's nothing else to examine may be right on the money except for one thing. The following questions:

"What about his family connection to slave owners in McComb, Mississippi? And "How deep does J. Edgar Hoover's root run into slavery?"

Millie answered, *"I'd say his roots into slavery goes as deep as the blue sea."*

In a phone call Curt Gentry admitted to Millie in a phone conversation more than a decade before he died, the one thing he overlooked was his family connections, which Millie had reminded him, and he responded,

"How could I have missed it?"

Millie answered by explaining to him the facts that J. Edgar Hoover did a great job of keeping his family **very private** from all outsiders.

So, what did Gentry miss in his research that Millie knew all too well? He overlooked information suggesting the real identity of this powerful man's biological father was not the man who everyone thought raised him. It all sounds interesting.

Many will say, could this supposed relationship to this man be just another trumped-up story? "A wild-goose chase?" Or could it be another kind of witch-hunt or an attention-getter?

Millie agrees that it could be all of that above, but she got the proof and witch-hunt? Not this time. We have the evidence, and oral history matching the documents with census records. It will be the first publication that lays out this public figure's complete background and his noticeable circumstances surrounding his birth about his family and bloodline connection to slaves.

Millie had a front seat to the gossip, rumors, and storytelling at family reunions in McComb, Mississippi where she grew up. There is no reason for her to single out one man living in D.C. or claim kinship to his family. Additionally, there is no motive to single out a man whom people in Millie's community, in general, had no respect for him. He hated all black people due to his fear of his secret being exposed "The One Drop Rule," accept, he had more than just one drop of black blood running through his veins.

Millie discovered the most, "Shocking Revelations regarding J. Edgar Hoover life!" His family connection to her slave great-great-grandmother, her Big Daddy, and was even more shocking when Millie discovered the real stories of the three slave women behind the birth of J. Edgar, and Clarence Allen his first cousin. Learning the entire history regarding the sexual encounters of those slave women was the bigger shock regarding the sexual-incest-raping by slave owners on the Hoover Plantation, which included truth and lies regarding these three women:

1.) A 16-year-old girl named Sarah was brought from West Africa to America to become a maid and was sold as a slave. 2.) Elizabeth Allen was Sarah's child born a slave. 3.) Emily Allen was Elizabeth child also born a slave. The truth was it did happen, and the lies were the denial, which became secrets.

"Three Powerful Women."

Millie said you would expect someone who was a blood relative to know personally and some intimate details about the family. Why? Well, if you are in the family, you are exposed to personal information at a family gathering that includes important time-dated achievements, birthday celebrations, family-pictures, school celebrations or college graduations, job promotions, the birth of a new baby, and weddings.

However, Millie never found any of that to have happened in J. Edgar Hoover's lifetime on any level with his white family. On the other hand, if there are skeletons in someone's closet somewhere hiding embarrassing family secrets, then they had to keep it hidden, which is what J. Edgar Hoover did his entire life, and so did many other family members. "They Passed for White!"

There is more about J. Edgar's private life in DC, in the next chapter.

Chapter 7

PRIVATE LIFE IN DC

In 2000 when this story about J. Edgar Hoover passing for a white hit in the news, the media, newspapers, and want to be Journalist were writing their stories depicting J. Edgar Hoover into whatever they could find regarding his work in the FBI. They didn't look into his family history. Many were skeptical, "Who in the world would believe that the son of a slave father would be the most powerful man in America?

However, Millie was quite intrigued by Kenneth D. Ackerman article he wrote on the subject of J. Edgar Hoover's life within his perspective.

Kenneth D. Ackerman wrote a paper on the myths regarding J. Edgar Hoover relating to some of Millie's previous work. Millie enjoyed reading Kenneth's article and wanted to share a few of his thoughts as she explains her thoughts regarding the article and her family's oral history told to her as a child.

"Despite rampant speculation — that

Hoover was gay, a cross-dresser or had no sex life — the truth about his sex life is nearly impossible to pin down." (Ackerman 2011)

Kenneth D. Ackerman's paper on J. Edgar Hoover was referring to J. Edgar's gay, cross-dresser, and his sex life did get discussed during Millie's childhood. She had comments as she debated. Take a look:

"I've heard that J. Edgar Hoover was a gay cross-dresser, but this wasn't revealed to me during our family discussions regarding the connection to him as a relative when I was a child. However, when I grew up, I learned about his gay cross-dressing, and the memories of the truth of him being a relative came back to me. Then about the "Gay Cross-Dressing" family members only said he would do and say anything to keep his connection to his black family a secret." Millie explained.

The Allen family knew what was the most critical thing to J. Edgar Hoover was keeping his secret safe. Millie did say she supposed getting married and bringing a child into their union could reveal some visual African genetic. In Millie's family, the black gene is active, and J. Edgar knew it, and he thought getting married would cause his secret to becoming even more apparent. He'd rather have a lifetime of being a bachelor or being gay was better than being black.

So, it's apparent J. Edgar settled on a lifetime relationship with his FBI associate director, Clyde Tolson and they both were lifelong bachelors together as lovers. It gave Hoover safety in his mind to continue to live in darkness hiding hid real heritage. To him, it seemingly worked because he lived his entire life as a gay man and nobody knew about his bloodline with African Americans slaves, not even his lover Clyde knew, not that he cared. In Millie's mind was this thought, and she spoke it,

"I think J. Edgar felt bringing bring gay into his life worked because the secret would never be uncovered? He had done everything he could to take this secret to his grave, but, a young black ten-year-old girl from McComb, Mississippi had heard the secret, and that girl was me."

In Millie's family oral storytelling during family reunions some family members did talk about J. Edgar Hoover having sexual relationships, but with famous white women. One, in particular, being "Marilyn Monroe. Now, this was menfolk talk! May have been just rumored. The stories were that Hoover was in love with her and it was his secret. However, one of Millie's uncles would say,

"Who wouldn't be in love with Marilyn Monroe," and they would all laugh out loud. As an adult now, Millie said,

"I think the men were just doing what they do when men are all together having a beer, and "talk trash."

J. Edgar Hoover kept files on all the presidents. He made it his business to hang around people that may rise to power and get to know all candidates that were running for any position in government, especially anyone running for

President. He would research their background looking for their secrets, while getting to know their family, friends, childhood teachers, and old girlfriends or boyfriends to dig up anything he could to hold over their heads in the future.

The one-big-drop of black blood running through J. Edgar Hoover's veins had him living in constant fear. He felt it necessary to develop a defense system that would protect him for the rest of his life. *Showing hatred toward his own people would be the key to fool us.* He considered this leverage and would search for the most incriminating evidence to reinforce his power over people. Some of the evidence a journalist named, Kenneth D. Ackerman wrote below about it in his paper regarding J. Edgar Hoover's power play:

> *"Harry Truman, Dwight D. Eisenhower, John F. Kennedy, and Richard Nixon all wanted to fire J. Edgar Hoover, but J. Edgar had his defense system in place regarding all of them; "Files of their wrongdoing." J. Edgar Hoover had worked hard building his image as a top-notch cop with the public, and in time many of them learn to trust him, but the black people were afraid of him."*
> (Ackerman 2011)

In the 1960s, when some black people started to become movie stars and to make money, he watched them by using his agents to set them up with crimes that they didn't commit. Also, any white politician or black leaders that wanted to build up hope within the black community were targeted, such as, President John F. Kennedy, Robert Kennedy, and Martin Luther King Jr.

J. Edgar Hoover set up Martin Luther King Jr. when he started wiretapping his hotel room to show his infidelity to his wife while he was traveling the country fighting for civil rights. J. Edgar Hoover wanted to destroy his life and break up Martin Luther King Jr.'s home, but he failed.

Then, Mr. Ackerman wrote,

"J. Edgar Hoover was close to President Franklin D. Roosevelt and Lyndon Johnson, because he had them in his control, so he thought. He used those files whenever he needed to have control with others such as, Supreme Court justices Felix Frankfurter and Louis Brandeis, movie stars Mary Pickford and Marilyn Monroe, first lady Eleanor Roosevelt, physicist Albert Einstein, Zionist leader Chaim Weizmann and philanthropist John D. Rockefeller III, among others — often replete with unconfirmed gossip about private sex lives and radical ties." (Ackerman 2011)

"By 1960, the FBI had open, "subversive" files on some 432,000 Americans. Hoover deemed the most sensitive files as "personal and confidential" and kept them in his office, where his secretary, Helen Gandy, could watch them. Today, with few exceptions, Hoover's FBI files are open for any American to see at the National Archives. They

do a fascinating reading and paint a stark portrait of power run amok." (Ackerman 2011)

All of the comments above in both paragraphs were stated in our history, but unless you were a relative, you wouldn't know J. Edgar Hoover's real fear. There were many more questions about this shocking revelation of J. Edgar Hoover and Millie's grandfather (Big Daddy) as relatives. What about Helen Gandy? Millie's family talked about her a lot during their storytelling, it was whispered that he was in love with her, but his fear of his African-American slave bloodline showing up in their children. So, she became his best friend and most trusted person in his life, other than Clyde Tolsen.

"Helen Gandy was an American Civil servant. She was the executive secretary to J. Edgar Hoover from 1921 until his death but started to work in the Justice office in 1918. So, Helen worked for him for 54 years. She was born in Rockville, NJ and she moved to Washington DC, at the age of 21. Helen went to Strayer Business College and then George Washington University Law School after moving to DC. She went to work in the Justice Department as a file clerk in 1918, and soon became a typist in Hoover's office.

In 1921 J. Edgar Hoover became the assistant director of the Bureau of Investigation, he requested that Helen come and work for him. J. Edgar Hoover trusted Helen. When he became the Director of the Bureau in 1924, Ms. Gandy was his trusted right hand and the only person he let safeguard his private life and the files he kept on influential people.

She was also, trusted with his information on his personal life with Clyde Tolsen, his lifelong companion. In 1972 after Hoover's death Helen was instructed to destroy all of his files and spent many hours doing what he requested. Helen retired after his death. She died of a heart attack July 13, 1988, and took all of Hoover' secrets to her grave.

There is so much more to uncover in the life of Mr. Hoover, and the Allen family. The next chapters Millie's story takes you through documents, census records, and the connection between the Allen's and the Hoover's. Then you can review the documents in the "Photo Album on pages in the back of the book.

Chapter 8

CENSUS RECORDS

Let's review the census records and documents found that connect J. Edgar Hoover to Big Daddy as first cousins. We will explain all the materials as well as reveal the census records.

After 21 years of excruciating and mind-boggling digging, they found the truth! True-life evidence of oral stories said to Millie validates their connection between her family and the Hoover family. The research is complete, and the proof is indisputable! Just follow Millie through the researched census records. If you follow the facts and you will be able to review all the documents and pictures in the photo album at the end of the story.

We have census records and vital birth recorded documents that were erased in the archives census records during J. Edgar's lifetime; it was rumors told to Millie by an FBI agent, that Hoover would send agents to the archives with typewriters to change his birth record. Well, Millie found documents in the archives/census that were tampered with concerning J. Edgar Hoover birth record.

"He will erase his records," said Big Daddy. It validates Millie's oral history.

Millie found census records in the identification column: W for White, B for Black, and the M for Mulatto," usually the census taker used those letter: W, B, or M. to identify what race a person was at birth.

Millie was not sure those are reliable, because she found her family listed incorrectly on occasions. The record she found showed William Allen as B for black and then changed to W for white, to say he was a White person and not Black.

Now that we understand those census records, we took a closer walk through the Allen's and the Hoover's documented lives. The presumption that J. Edgar's mother, Anna was of European stock was purely made up to hide the reality that his mother was born into slavery, and sold to Dickerson N. Hoover. The oral history and the documents we found corroborate those facts. That would, of course, explain why nothing was discovered about her ancestries in the archives, or any other materials, such as the names of her mother father, brothers, sisters, uncles, aunts or even cousins. If her parents were of European birth, that knowledge wouldn't be difficult to acquire, especially for a person claiming to be Caucasian.

Millie ordered these records for J. Edgar Hoover, and they were received in our care as a certified copy of his Certificate of Birth signed and sealed by Carl W. Wilson the "Registrar" on July 21, 2000.

This is what was in the records, J. Edgar's brother; Dickerson gave a false statement before a notary at the time of the filing for J. Edgar Hoover's birth records. Dickerson Jr., appears in a photo with his parents Dickerson Naylor Hoover Sr., and mother, Annie Hoover.

J. Edgar used that photo as his identity in Curt Gentry's book because he would look more like a white boy with his parents. At the time of this photo, J. Edgar wasn't born yet, and Dickerson Jr. was five years old in the picture.

After finding these documents, Millie wanted to understand more about what Big Daddy had told me about J. Edgar's birth records. We discovered that there were not any birth records found in 1895 on file for J. Edgar Hoover at the time of his birth or after his birth that year.

It was 1957 when Millie was told he was related to her and she would not be able to find any birth certificate of his birth in 1895. J. Edgar was the head of the FBI for God sake and had no birth records. How can that be? What is up with our system that this was allowed? The answer is clear; he was a black man according to the "One Drop Rule."

During Millie's research of his birth records, she wondered why he was trying so hard to obtain his birth certificate at the age of 44? And, why didn't he have birth records before his parent's death? Then she thought, "Could it be because of our laws concerning passports? When did we have to have passports?" Those were a lot of questions, but all were on Millie's mind. She decided to research those questions, starting with passports.

The information Millie found was fascinating and helped her understand the reasoning behind what J. Edgar Hoover was trying to do. He knew his entire life that he had no real proof of his birth; and caused him to do unlawful things to get his passport, to continue his work, even if he had to falsify records with lies.

Well, this is what all Americans had to do regarding Passports to travel out of the country, and we all had to have our birth certificates starting back to the early 1900s. Also, during World War I (1914–1918,) the European countries introduced the *"Passport"* to their citizens. This was done for the "Travel Control Act of May 22, 1918" which permitted the United States president to proclaim a *"Passport"* law requirement while we were at war. President Wilson proclaimed on August 18, 1918, for all American citizens to get a passport. Then during the time of May 22, 1918 -1921, after the end of World War I to travel to any country outside of the United States a passport was required by all citizens who enabled them to leave and return into the state.

Later during the time of June 21, 1941 -1945 after the end of World War II it was reinforced with stronger rules for our citizens to travel out and back in the country. This made it clear to Millie why J. Edgar Hoover was trying to get his records in order in 1938.

Doctoring the Documents (J. Edgar Hoover's doctored birth records will be shown in the photo album in the back of this book.) One of the strangest documents ever seen in the archives was J. Edgar Hoover's birth recording.

Millie noticed that each new birth record within this document she found had identical information, except for J. Edgar's. Each parent had a number, and those numbers are pretty much in order, except for J. Edgar's number. In review of J. Edgar's birth records, it was apparent it was added some years later, after his actual birth. Listed below are the actual birth records typed legibly for better viewing and understanding. However, the actual document will be in the photo album at the end of the book.

Hooks, William & Annie	67834
Hoover, Clayton & Maggie	72632
Hooke, Franci J & Maggie	88300
Hoover, William H & Mary A	88688
Hoover, Dickerson N. & Annie M.	419530
John Edgar 1-1-95 m –w (male – white)	

That was how records were kept back in the 1800s. This is a census document that was doctored as J. Edgar Hoover's name was added, 43 years later out of sequence.

They found the record called, Record of a Birth that should have been filed in 1895 when J. Edgar was born. Deceitfully, J. Edgar and his brother filed it on September 21, 1938. The document will be shown to you later in the photo album.

J. Edgar's Certificate of Birth was filed September 17, 1938, by J. Edgar and his brother Dickerson N. Hoover. Dickerson N. Hoover, the white father, died March 30, 1921, and Anna Hoover, the mother, died on February 24, 1938. These records validate the oral history told regarding the connection between Allen's (my family) and the Hoovers. J. Edgar Hoover's brother Dickerson Jr., decided to help his brother cover up his birth date and agreed to sign a legal document stating J. Edgar Hoover was his bother and he witnessed J. Edgar's home birth when he was fifteen years old. Below is the exact wording that was written on the document:

> "I, Dickerson N. Hoover, of Glenn Dale, Maryland, son of Dickerson N. Hoover, and Annie S. Hoover, depose and say that I was present at the birth of and know of my own knowledge that my brother, John Edgar Hoover, was born in the home of our parents, 413 Seward Square, Southeast, Washington, D.C., on January 1, 1895. At the time of John Edgar Hoover's birth I was 15 years of age." SEAL.

They noticed in reviewing, "The DC Department of Health's Vital birth Records" filed by J. Edgar and his brother in 1938, there was no doctor signed on the document when J. Edgar Hoover was born in 1895.

They also observed a question on the document asking if J. Edgar was "legitimate, the question was; Yes or No? The answer selected was No, which meant J. Edgar Hoover was an illegitimate child, just what the oral history stated. J. Edgar Hoover's "Certificate of Birth" was a perfect match to the oral story told by "Big Daddy." All documents are posted in the photo portion of this book for your review.

Now in reviewing the census records, Millis found more about the love affair between Ivery Hoover and Anna, J. Edgar's mother. In the Washington DC 1900s census document they found this listed: Dickerson Hoover, with his wife Anna M., his son Dickerson Jr., age 19, his daughter Lillian, age 17, and a small boy listed as John E., age 5. This was the first time J. Edgar Hoover was listed in the census records as a child.

These records are proof to the Allen and Hoover Oral History. It is hard to find oral stories matching census documents, but Millie did. She found in the 1900s census of Pike County Mississippi listed: Ivery Hoover living in the house with his black wife and their children in the 1900s census.

Ten years later we found in the 1910s census of Pike County Mississippi records listed: Ivy Hoover as head of
104

household with a white wife named Anna Hoover, with his and Arie's children. Millie noticed that the census keepers didn't always spell Ivery Hoover's name as it was by the family, we found it spelled "Ivy" and "Ivery in many documents." So, Ivy-or-Ivery, are "one-and-of-the-same" going forward. The recorded documents show a clear connection to J. Edgar Hoover to his real family. The census history clearly shows Millie's family as the blood relatives to J. Edgar Hoover family. It proves the rumors of a scorching love affair between Ivy Hoover and Dickerson N. Hoover wife Anna Hoover; J. Edgar Hoover's mother.

This record found in the 1910s census records in Washington, DC, was a huge find; we noticed that Anna was not found nor Dickerson N. Hoover, and there was no census record filed for the Dickerson Hoover family, with his wife, Anna, in 1910 nor a boy John E., who would be age 15 in 1910. Nor any record with Dickerson Jr. and Sister Lillian listed in the family census in DC. Why? It could have been because the older children Dickerson Jr., and Lillian were head of their households during the 1910s census, but what about their parents and J. Edgar who was 15? Maybe he was left in DC with his brother or sister.

We searched and found that her Husband Dickerson Hoover was in the sanitarian hospital in DC when the 1910s census was recorded. Which is why Anna was having an affair with Ivy/Ivery, she had moved into the house in Mississippi with Ivery, since Arie had left Ivy after finding out about the love affair, and the child J. Edgar Hoover. We searched again for Anna in the 1910 Washington, DC census and the family records were nowhere to be found.

This census record of the 1910s proves what had been rumored during the oral family story regarding the love affair between Anna Hoover and Ivery Hoover. Uncle Ivery was having a love affair and at the same time having sex with his wife. Arie Ivery's wife was having children every year with him except for 1895. Anna got pregnant by Uncle Ivery, and the baby was born in 1895, which was J. Edgar. Uncle Ivery's wife got pregnant with Mozilla who was born in 1896. Then Uncle Ivery's wife Arie found out about the child and affair. She left him with all the children in 1910. Then Anna moved in with her lover and his/Arie's children.

So, the 1910s census recorded Anna as Ivery's wife and all of Arie's children living in the same house. When J. Edgar grew-up and at the age of 22 he had threatened Ivery if he didn't let his mother go back to DC with Dickerson. The family said that Ivery tried to reason with J. Edgar as his father, but it didn't work. Then Ivery was found dead, and family members said he was murdered by J. Edgar's orders on November 18, 1917, only six days before his 42nd birthday.

Arie Hoover remarried just 11 months after the death of Ivery Hoover. We found the Marriage License of Sylvester Bullock and Arie Hoover on December 23, 1918.

The documented history regarding the three slave women of the Allen family lived a life that was just unbelievable, but Millie understood and she accepted their sacrifice for enduring such an abusive life for the future of the family. It also helped the women in Millie's family become strong. She found the documented real life-story of those three slave women who were the root of her family very inspiring.

They established hope within the future and helped Millie find peace within sharing a glance into how her great-grandmothers were sexually abused/incest as bed-warmers-slave-women during their lives. So, within the following pages of, "Shocking Truth Lies," join Millie in a glance into their lives.

Millie's grandmother Lydia Allen, her daughters, and their daughter were strong women going into the future from the backs of those women; *Sarah, Elizabeth, and Emily.* In the next chapters, we will enter into the life of those three women, who were an essential part of our family,

The storytelling concerning the Allen and Hoover's family's beginning was 'thought-provoking,' and sharing the documented history of Millie's origin regarding those three women was a big historical discovery.

Chapter 9

MISSISSIPPI FAMILY CENSUS

Now we are going to take a look at what we found in the research about Clarence Allen (Big Daddy) her grandfather and his family. Millie was excited when she discovered her Big Daddy's signature on his Army papers in the census library in Salt Lake City. He was in his early twenties when he went into the Army. She also found his marriage certificate, showing he was married to Litta Neal. Her name was changed somewhere in time to Lydia, or the census keepers just spelled what they heard. So, Millie called her Big Mama Litta, but Lydia was her name, maybe that is why the census keepers spelled her name Litta.

Clarence Allen (Big Daddy), and Litta (aka Lydia) were married on December 23, 1915. Rev W.m. Campbell performed the ceremony. The witnesses were Big Daddy's sister Florence and J. M. Holmes. Clarence and Lydia had sixteen children, and Millie's mother was one of them.

The researchers found copies of other family members' marriage certificates were also located, such as Aunt Ruth, Lucile, and pictures of Big Daddy, his sisters, and his father. There were family records of William Allen, born in February of 1870, the son of William Hoover born

1832. William Allen married a woman named Elizabeth Haynes, born in November of 1870, and the researchers found their pictures. They were excited and proud to see those documents regarding Millie's descendants, and some she knew in her lifetime. There were documents showing William Allen and Elizabeth Haynes her great-grandparents of Pike County, Mississippi, and they were the parents of these three children:

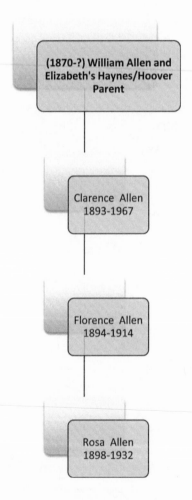

Our Oral History was documented in the records as it was told to Millie. She read Curt Gentry's book entitled "J. Edgar Hoover: The Man and The Secrets." In this book, she read about a William Allen in Washington, DC, who worked for the FBI. Then in the same book, she noticed that there were two other unusual names. They were family names like Robert Hoover and George Allen. Relatives? Maybe!

J. Edgar Hoover had a sister named Lillian Hoover. Millie had an aunt named Lillian Allen, who lived in McComb, MS, but she has passed. J. Edgar Hoover's family connection with the Mississippi Allen family is now confirmed. Ivery Hoover and William Allen, who were Millie's Big Daddy's father, were very close and more like best friends than brothers, Millie's mother reported. Now let's take a look into documented records regarding Ivery Hoover's family tree:

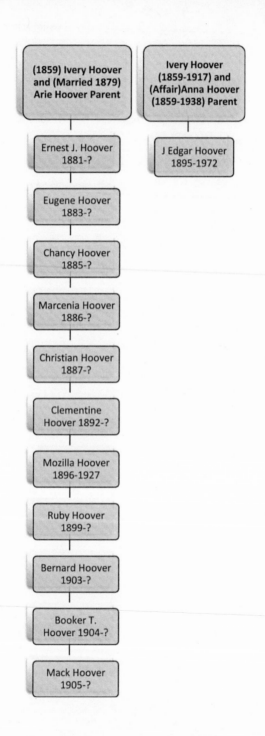

(1859) Ivery Hoover and (Married 1879) Arie Hoover Parent

Ivery Hoover (1859-1917) and (Affair)Anna Hoover (1859-1938) Parent

Ernest J. Hoover 1881-?

J Edgar Hoover 1895-1972

Eugene Hoover 1883-?

Chancy Hoover 1885-?

Marcenia Hoover 1886-?

Christian Hoover 1887-?

Clementine Hoover 1892-?

Mozilla Hoover 1896-1927

Ruby Hoover 1899-?

Bernard Hoover 1903-?

Booker T. Hoover 1904-?

Mack Hoover 1905-?

After Ivery started his affair with Anna Hoover and Arie found out she finally left home, leaving him and her children, and rumors had started all over the town that Anna Hoover had left her husband in DC, and moved in with Ivery and his children.

Millie heard about Arie too and researched showed those rumors and oral history to be true. The researcher found Anna in the 1910 census records living with Ivery, and Arie's children. Later, she found out that her husband was in the hospital with some mental health breakdown.

The researchers discovered Clarence Allen was enumerated as a seven-year-old in the 1900 U.S. census of Pike County Mississippi. It was noted that the children had a limited amount of formal education. They worked on the farm. Millie's grandfather Big Daddy signed his draft registration card, and marriage license with a signature rather than an "X," although he was illiterate since there were other legal papers discovered with the signature page marked with X.

Millie wasn't surprised about the illiteracy she found in the research among the family due to how education was viewed in regards to Black people in slavery. What was so refreshing to her was how the people that survived through slavery viewed education so differently due to being forbidden to read during slavery. Today Millie can see how important education is for the Black children moving forward.

According to the memory of the Oral history, Millie's grandfather Clarence Allen who was born in Lincoln County fathered all sixteen children with my grandmother Litta (Lydia). The children were born and raised on the homestead property until a fire destroyed it twice, and it was rumored that they were being burned out because a white family wanted the land. Some people said, later there were tax problems, and they lost the property forever. Well, Millie discovered the true facts, during her research and that wasn't true. The recorded deed showed Millie's Big Daddy, sold the land, for $1200, because he was tired of getting burned out. It wasn't safe for his family living there anymore. He took the money, which was a substantial amount of money back in that time and he built a new home for his family in the city of McComb with his own hands.

Millie grandfather Big Daddy was a very talented man; he built that big house himself. He also built lots of other homes in McComb, Mississippi. He was a gentle good man and wanted to be a better man than the men he observed during his childhood, and he was a great man to Millie.

The men she watched growing up were different, and we will take a look into the lives of "Black men and White men during slavery."

Chapter 10

HIDDEN IN PLAIN SIGHT

As far as J. Edgar's mother was concerned, the family's oral history stated that she was handpicked by Dickerson N. Hoover, from the Mississippi plantation. He took Anna to Washington DC to marry, and she passed for white. She was born on the Hoover plantation and called a half-breed, and her parent's identity was a secret. It was the reason why the researchers could not find her ancestry.

Anna Hoover was born 1859, which was the same year Ivery Hoover was born. Anna was a beautiful woman, which is why Dickerson N. Hoover wanted her as his wife. She was J. Edgar Hoover's mother. Dickerson N. Hoover was born in 1856. He was older than Ivery and Anna.

Our family oral history stated that Dickerson N. Hoover was visiting the plantation in Mississippi, and couldn't take his eyes off Anna. He knew about William Hoover, one of Christian Hoover's brothers who had found his wife Elizabeth Allen on the plantation in Mississippi and purchased her to become his white-wife. Then returned to DC, where they married.

Having the same mindset, Dickerson N. Hoover thought he could take Anna back to DC, marry her, and they could live happily forever. Little that he knew, Anna had a lover on the plantation, however, that didn't matter to the slave owner since she had to do what the slave owner her master told her. She was sold to Dickerson N. Hoover and taken back to DC. He was very proud, and as a man of class, with wealth in a white man's society, he expected Anna to pass as of white heritage.

Some sources have stated that Anna Hoover was of European extraction, but can't validate it by any historians. However, the claim was lacking any documentation. Since J. Edgar Hoover was trying to hide his real roots, he possibly put that information into the records to change the real truth.

In Millie's oral history account of J. Edgar Hoover's mother was found to be more accurate stating Anna was a mulatto slave. This position matches the word-of-mouth history that seems the most reliable at this point regarding Anna Hoover.

Let's ask a few questions,

"Has anybody ever seen pictures of J. Edgar Hoover as a child or adult celebrating his birthday with Anna, Dickerson or his siblings? Has his family attended any of his awards dinners? Are there any pictures of them with J. Edgar as a young child at any place, such as the zoo, park, movie, or shopping?"

Those questions were of concern by many people who attended functions with him. J. Edgar Hoover spoke of his parents when he was being interviewed by Curt Gentry when he was writing a book about him, and he lied to Curt. He gave Curt a family picture of Dickerson Sr., Anna, and Dickerson Jr. at five years old, and told Curt it was him as a young boy.

J. Edgar Hoover was trying to create himself a family; only he couldn't, because he didn't belong. No one saw him attend his father or mother's funeral after his or her death, or it wasn't in the news. Nor, were there family pictures of him with his siblings, Dickerson Jr. and his sister Lillian Hoover.

Millie found pictures of J. Edgar in her mother's family collection of photographs she got from "Big Daddy" her grandfather's house after they passed. It was pictures of J. Edgar as a young boy, and Millie didn't know who the little light skin boy was until she asked her mother.

Millie's mother during storytelling said Dickerson N. Hoover had a lot of hatred toward the young J. Edgar, due to his wife's affair with Ivery, and he wouldn't have anything to do with J. Edgar as a child. He refused to take any picture with him as a child, or even let himself be photographed with J. Edgar.

We found this statement in the Gentry biography book, "J. Edgar Hoover; The Man and The Secret," on page 116. It states, "Considering the meteoric rise, Hoover should have been happy, but he was sad. There are reasons to believe he wasn't in 1917 and was asked; you look sad, and why aren't you happy, since you were just Promoted? He said, "My father died."

Well, guess which one of his fathers died in 1917? Dickerson N. Hoover died in 1921, and Ivery Hoover died in 1917!

There were many severe flaws in his character and his professional performance on many occasions, but everyone was afraid of him. J. Edgar Hoover was not scared to get his hands dirty no matter what's asked of him or he felt he needed to do whatever it took to protect his deep dark secret. He was a spiteful man that was happy soaring personal hatreds toward the black people. J. Edgar Hoover made it clear of his hostility toward Martin Luther King Jr. He had to be hard-pressed into hiring black agents for the bureau, and even then he hired a black agent he could manipulate. He tapped the telephones of Government officials on request; however, a lot of it was for his use to protect himself and get more leverage over the legal system and he inspected files of politicians without their knowledge to have power over them in the future.

FBI agent, Mont Wesley Swearingen, who became a friend to Millie during the time of the research of this book, he said many FBI agents felt J. Edgar Hoover was of mixed race and he was trying to hide it by spreading out so much hatred toward the Black race. Mont Wesley Swearingen was born May 20, 1927; Steubenville, Ohio was a former FBI Special Agent from 1951 to 1977. He has authored several books, *FBI Secrets*, and *To Kill a President*, an examination of the John F. Kennedy assassination. Mr.

Swearingen was on Millie's team during her research in Washington, DC. They found a special bond and worked together for over ten years.

When J. Edgar Hoover talks of his hostility toward the Black race, Dick Gregory always said, "You Black Yourself." It was clear J. Edgar Hoover did everything he could to hide the fact that he was illegitimate and a child with that "One Drop Rule," started back in slavery. The one drop of black blood running through your veins meant you are not pure, but damaged goods.

God forbid if J. Edgar Hoover had been discovered having one drop of black blood! It was why J. Edgar Hoover tried so hard to look white his entire life. He even presented the picture show in our photo album page of his parents with his brother Dickerson Jr. to deceive people of his identity in place of his brother, because there were no pictures of him anywhere with his parents found. Why did Dickerson N. Hoover refuse to take photos with J. Edger or have anything to do with him as a father?

What About J. Edgar's Brother and Sister?

J. Edgar grew up with one brother, Dickerson Naylor Hoover Jr., and one sister, Lillian Hoover. In a time when birth control pills didn't exist, J. Edgar was born more than a decade after his siblings. J. Edgar Hoover's half-brother Dickerson Jr. was 14 years older than J. Edgar and his sister Lillian was 12 years older. But still Dickerson Jr. claimed he was 15 years old at the time of J. Edgar's birth; he was trying to help J. Edgar get his birth certificate.

In the research, they found that by 1917 his sister, Lillian was ill. At this time Dickerson Jr., age 36, and 22 years old J. Edgar became the family's sole supporters. Their parents would have been up into their 60s.

J. Edgar Hoover's Mother, Anna M Hoover died on February 24, 1938. Then, on June 24, 1938, J. Edgar was enjoying a day with young actress Shirley Temple. It was interesting to know that his mother had just died February of 1938, then by September 17, 1938, J. Edgar Hoover was rushing through Washington DC with his brother Dickerson trying to get his birth certificate legalized as a white man, and June 24, 1938, he's out celebrating with a young actress.

https://tucson.com/shirley-temple-and-hoover/image_c24477d6-931e-11e3-be14-001a4bcf887a.html

Mind you, when Millie reviewed the 1890 census regarding the fire in the basement of the Commerce Building in Washington D.C., priceless family records were destroyed. Documents that contained vital family statistics, that links to many heritages, now had disappeared from the Government files. The majority of the 1890 documents' population schedules got severely damaged by fire in the Commerce Department Building in January 1921.

How suspicious this fire was on January 10, 1921, and the death of Dickerson Naylor Hoover on March 30, 1921, which was just a few months after the burning of vital records pointing to the deep dark secret that would disgrace his family, because some of the documents survived the fire. What timing! Was that a coincidence? It was clear to the Allen family that Dickerson N. Hoover wasn't ever going to be happy if the secret of his wife having an illegitimate child by an African-American man ever came to light. It was clear to J. Edgar his stepson.

The researcher and Millie believed, even after Ivery's untimely death, still such a young man, J. Edgar always wanted to belong to his white side of his family and would do anything to keep his dark secret dead and buried with his biological father, who was Ivery Hoover. Did J. Edgar set that fire to please his white father? Millie believes that J. Edgar Hoover wanted Dickerson N. Hoover to love him, accept him, and be proud of him before they both died. And he would have done anything to make that happen.

Who set the fire?

J. Edgar or his brokenhearted stepfather Dickerson N. Hoover who couldn't bear the shame of his wife's infidelity, and bringing a black child into his life. There were rumors in the Allen family that J. Edgar Hoover set the fire. Dickerson N. Hoover had one last plea to keep his family's reputation in good standing, and someone had to burn the census records with that family history. The 1890 Census records were vital to Americans. Millie read this article below,

> *"In the United States residents completed millions of detailed questionnaires, yet only a fragment of the general population schedules and an incomplete set of special schedules enumerating Union veterans and widows are available today.*

Reference sources routinely dismiss the 1890 census records as "destroyed by fire" in 1921. Examination of the records of the Bureau of Census and other federal agencies, however, reveals a far more complex tale. It was a genuine tragedy of records-played out before Congress fully established a National Archives--and eternally anguishing to researchers." (Blake 1996)

It was attractive to Millie because it was clear that the 1890 census had vital information about J. Edgar Hoover's heritage that would connect him to the Allen family. Also, the fire hurt a lot of people who needed to find their family heritage connections were gone. It was a selfish act on the part of J. Edgar Hoover; to start a fire to hide your deep dark secret, and destroy records of millions of other Americans chance to find their roots. However, Millie and her researcher still was able to discover enough to see the oral history of damaged, changed, and burned records to get to the truth.

Oral History can be as compelling as documented history. It's like listening to storytelling, reviewing a movie, and looking at the family pictures.

This fire of census records was exactly what Big Daddy told his ten-year-old granddaughter, Millie; this was oral history repeated in documents. The "Census Fire "1921", and J. Edgar Hoover's father Dickerson N. Hoover's death "1921", just one month and twenty days after the attempt to burn family history records there were rumors in the family, "He did it." Thank God, they weren't all destroyed." That was great because Millie found what Big Daddy told her right in the documents.

However, many Blacks and Whites utilized oral history (word-of-mouth), to preserve that history for generations. Due to the fire things changed with the way our census records were kept and reported. Up until the 1840s, only names of heads of households were required on census reports. As things changed the census records kept improving, the population spiraled upward.

By the time of the 1880s Census everyone living in an American home, including former slaves (slavery had ended), would be reported by name. It resulted in a more accurate accounting of homes throughout the country, including immigrants and the languages they spoke. It proved extremely valuable for everyone trying to trace his or her ancestry.

If others discover their ancestry, and some of the ancestors may be slaves just as Millie's family. She hoped they would feel the spirit of their ancestors as she did.

J. Edgar Hoover had his goals in life to pursue influential people, and he did everything in his power to hide this area of his life. His efforts were successful as long as he lived, but what he didn't know was, his first cousin would tell his ten-year-old granddaughter the hidden secret.

Unfortunately, J. Edgar's life was a trap he couldn't escape no matter how hard he tried to hide his true identity.

And try he did, the little ten-year-old girl knew the truth. She discovered the records and documents that matched the oral history of the Allen's. She kept digging beneath the surface of one of the most controversial issues, and everything verbal spoken and documented word found its way into their lives today.

In the latter part of the 19th century, the foundation was firmly laid for young John Edgar Hoover's rise to power. But, he needed to get past one infinite obstacle he didn't know about: "A ten-year-old little girl named Millie!"

Mr. Gregory was respected in the black community and was an advocate for human rights. He didn't know anything about J. Edgar's ethnicity for a fact, but he knew of the gestures and appearances of a black person. As he walked through the streets saying out loud concerning J. Edgar Hoover, "You Black Yourself," after many of J. Edgar's attacks on TV about Dr. Martin L. King, and it was mostly due to his appearances. Millie had an opportunity to speak with Mr. Gregory and introduced her family history to him, and she remembers what he said, "I'm not surprised, but you would have to be born in Mississippi to be related to J. Edgar Hoover."

There were others that agreed with Mr. Gregory, such as: Reverend Al Sharpton, Martin Luther King Jr., his wife Coretta Scott King, President Jack Kennedy, Senator Ted Kennedy, Senator Robert Kennedy, President Lyndon Johnson, John Lewis, Stokely Carmichael, and Reverend Jesse Jackson, James Forman, Reverend Ralph Abernathy, and many FBI Agents such as M. Wesley Swearingen. And many others suspected J Edgar Hoover was of mixed race, but many were afraid to speak of it for fear they could be killed. However, today many of them have passed on, and Millie did have the opportunity to speak with many of them after finishing her research in 2000, and those that saw her discovery and research was not surprised.

The next chapter is called "Blinding Fear, "and it starts with Millie discussing the movie "J. Edgar" because it portrayed J. Edgar Hoover and having a fear of his repressed sex life. Millie saw it differently.

Chapter 11

BLINDING FEAR

In the movie, "J. Edgar" Director Clint Eastwood states,

"J. Edgar Hoover led a deeply repressed sexual life; living with his mother until he was 40, awkwardly rejecting the attention of women and pouring his emotional, and at times, physical attention on his handsome deputy at the Federal Beau of Investigations."

Why do you think J. Edgar Hoover was so afraid to live his life openly and freely? Could it have been because he was ashamed of whom he really was? Not because he was homosexual, but because of the one-drop rule, admitting he was a Black man could have gotten him killed
.

Ancestry family records on Anna M. Hoover were challenging to find because of her bi-racial (Mulatto) heritage. Photos of her were found in documents presented by J. Edgar Hoover. When Millie reviewed the images carefully, she found one picture of J. Edgar Hoover's mother with her husband Dickerson. She was pretty and very young. The images were puzzling because they looked just like a very pretty Mariah Carey when Anna was young on the plantation.

"Why didn't Anna help J. Edgar Hoover get his birth records before she died if he lives with her until he was 40 years old, as stated in the movie by Clint Eastwood?

There were descendants from Emily still living in McComb, Mississippi where Millie was born. Millie had a chance to meet them and noticed that the grandchildren of Mozilla Hoover were still afraid of the memory of what happened to her. They were told the horrific tale of how she lost her life trying to be honest, and tell her half-brother's biological secret.

Well, remember, John T. Hoover, he was born in 1840 on the Hoover plantation in Mississippi, the oral story stated. He grew up and owned his slaves at a young age after being taken to the Maryland/DC area. Emily, who was a slave, was also his slave half-sister, according to research and oral history. We found documents in the archives as well as census records that confirm the oral history. We found a fascinating article written about a Black American slave form of a newspaper clipping, just as written, and it stated:

> "District of Columbia Free Negro Registers 1821-1861 copy of letter to John Hoover from Thomas Sewell of Baltimore: Sewell Rites that he is sorry to hear that Henry Brown has been jailed as a runaway slave. He has known Brown for 15 years and employed him as a butcher, and believes that he is free. Brown has a wife in Baltimore who says that he was born free. She has gone to Mr. Burrows to obtain a certificate of freedom for her husband, "but the notice being so short that I had this evidence cannot be produced in time [e] for your Brother." Sewell further states that you will run no risk of letting him out of jail until he can furnish sufficient evidence of his freedom (18 Oct. 1836). John Hoover appears before a justice of the peace and swears that he has known the Henry Brown mentioned in

Sewell's letter for the last three years and that he has passed as a free man. He also states that he knows Thomas Sewell and that Sewell is a man who can be relied on 19 October 1836.

Millie shared that newspaper article to show that John Hoover demonstrated in 1840 in our family history records was a relative who owned slaves. He was the slave girl Emily Allen's half-brother; they shared the same mother, Elizabeth Allen.

Now, what about J. Edgar Hoover's white father, and where was he when his wife was having an affair in Mississippi in 1917. On April 5, 1917, the day before war was declared, he was forced to resign his $2000 a year job with the U.S. Coast and Geodetic Survey. Dickerson N. Hoover was still alive in 1917 when Ivery Hoover was murdered or found dead in his home. The records showed Dickerson was in a hospital suffering from a condition that the doctors characterized as alternating moods of irritability, and inconsolable sadness. It is why we couldn't find their family in the census records in 1910 as a family in Washington DC.

"J. Edgar Hoover obtained terrifying power at an amazingly young age, just two years after graduating from college. His rise was rapid. The Justice Department was understaffed at the time, and many of its young men were enlisted in the military were only one part of the reason. His superiors were impressed; so impressed that less than three months after his arrival in 1917 he was promoted, and three months later, promoted again. By the age of 22 John Edgar

Hoover had found his niche in life. He had become a hunter of men.

> In the book authored by Curt Gentry, this is clearly documented: "In February 1919 Attorney General Thomas Gregory submitted his resignation. The next to leave was A. Bruce Fielaski, who was replaced as Chief of the Bureau of Investigation by William E. Allen." (Gentry 1991)

William Allen served as chief of the Bureau of Investigation for a short time in DC. It was less than six months before he was lost in the cracks of most Bureau histories.

The Allen's oral history stated; a family member appointed J. Edgar Hoover to the Bureau. The author's great-grandfather and uncle were named William Allen. He was the son of William Hoover. In regards to oral history, Millie listened and researched that J. Edgar Hoover got positioned in the FBI so well due to family in high places. The oral family stories said,

> "The oral story stated, William Hoover started the organization of investigation in his home, having meetings with selected men in high places, and he was the president of the Bureau of Investigations in the 1800s."

So, it was easy to place J. Edgar Hoover in position to someday become head of the FBI. He didn't need a birth certificate at that time because his family started the organization in the back rooms of their homes; stated inside the Allen family oral history. It was the biggest reason why J. Edgar Hoover was so adamant about never being moved from his position as "Director of the FBI" he felt he was entitled. One of J. Edgar's first assignments in 1917 was collecting secret files on Americans. By the time he was 27, he was the director of the Bureau of Investigations, which is now called the FBI. He held on to that position for nearly half a century.

J. Edgar Hoover allowed almost no one in his home. His secretary, Helen Gandy, was one of the few he allowed. She began working with him when he was only 22, and continued after his death. She started destroying records after his death even before government officials could look at them. J. Edgar himself began destroying files a year before he died.

Only two black people were allowed into his home; driver, James Crawford who was a handyman at his house (even after retiring) and a maid. J. Edgar never married and declared that he would never have children. He was afraid of showing his African American genes. Therefore, J. Edgar Hoover grew up hiding his ancestry. He hated himself. After the death of his step-father, he became his mother's only companion and sole support. J. Edgar left most of his estate to his long-time partner, Clyde Tolson. He was not close to his brother and sister. When he died, he cut his siblings and their children out of his will.

Chapter 12

J. EDGAR'S DEATH & LIFE

While looking for J. Edgar Hoover's obituary, this is what Millie found in many places shown below. Millie was hoping to find an obituary that showed who was left to mourn his death or what part of the family did he have a relationship with when he was alive. Also, she hoped to see his nieces and nephews listed as his living relatives, because his half-sister Lillian and Half-brother Dickerson may have had a few children. However, this is what she found representing his obituary:

"J. Edgar Hoover, 77, Dies; Will Lie in State in Capitol
https://www.biography.com/people/herbert-hoover-9343371

By FRED P. GRAHAM - MAY 3, 19

> "WASHINGTON, May 2—J. Edgar Hoover, who directed the Federal Bureau of Investigation for 48 years and built it into a dominant and controversial force in American law enforcement, died during the night from the effects of high blood pressure.

Mr. Hoover, who at 77 years of age still held the F.B.I. firmly within his control, died in his bedroom after working a full day in his office yesterday. His housekeeper found him at 8:30 this morning, slumped on the floor beside his bed.

His home is near Rock Creek Park in the northwest section of Washington.

Dr. James L. Luke, Washington's Medical Examiner, attributed the death to "hypertensive cardio - vascular disease." He said that Mr. Hoover had been suffering from a heart ailment for some time but gave no details.

He said that death could have been caused by heart failure associated with high blood pressure, but that no autopsy would be performed because the death was known to be due to natural causes.

Acting Attorney General Richard G. Kleindienst announced the death at 11 A.M., after F.B.I. offices around the world had been given the news and reports of it began to circulate here. Congress promptly voted its permission for his body to lie in state in the Capitol Rotunda—an honor accorded to only 21 persons before, of which eight were Presidents or former Presidents." (GRAHAM 1972)

Millie said,

"I was hoping to find something significant about his family ties or connection to his faith regarding family. I researched to find J. Edgar Hoover's, Obituary, but I found his resume like the one written by Fred P. Graham, and like the articles below written by the Bureau."

J. Edgar Hoover, Former Director of the Federal Bureau of Investigation

"John Edgar Hoover was an American law enforcement administrator and the first Director of the Federal Bureau of Investigation of the United States. He was appointed as the director of the Bureau of Investigation – the FBI's predecessor – in 1924 and was instrumental in founding the FBI in 1935, where he remained a director for over 37 years until his death in 1972 at the age of 77. Hoover has been credited with building the FBI into a larger crime-fighting agency than it was at its inception and with instituting a number of modernizations to police technology, such as a centralized fingerprint file and forensic Laboratories." (FBI 1972)

In researching his obituary Millie found several biographies of J. Edgar's work was found of all of his accomplishments, but nothing about his family connection as an obituary usually appears when a person expires. Millie personally considered what she found his accolades and not an Obituary. However, there was nothing in his so-called "Memorial" about his family, not anything, such as information regarding his mother, father, brother, sister, aunts, uncles, nieces, nephew, or even a close family

136

friends? These would be expected from his childhood. Doesn't that seem strange? Why? The most likely explanation was his biological family (of mixed race of course), were people he was ashamed of and could not be publically revealed. They were African-American slaves in Mississippi and many Caucasian Hoover family members that came out of the South/North Carolina and Mississippi that were still living in 1972 when he died.

This part of the research saddened Millie the most. She found herself feeling the weight and needless pain he bared because of his fear of being different. He had a unique opportunity to fight for people of all races and perhaps advocate change. He had the power in his hands to do something remarkable for the world. Millie believed that if he had told his own truth in 1970 himself, it would have empowered his life so much until he would have lost all the fear of having a part in African-American heritage.

When Millie was growing up in Mississippi as a little girl, she watched and was aware of J. Edgar's great anger with Rev. Martin L. King Jr. It was because of the love and attention that MLK got from the people. He gave hope that one day we will all be looked upon as, "One people."

Millie decided to have a look into President Herbert Hoover's family life and didn't see how he was connected to their Hoover's. She found that President Herbert Hoover was born in 1874 and died in the year 1964. However, noticing that he had an obituary of his death, and he had family members listed on his obituary. If you google search his life you will see his wonderful family. His records are easily found in the census and information regarding his family. She noticed he was born 21 years before J. Edgar Hoover. Millie was searching for his obituary, to see if he was related to J. Edgar Hoover, because some family members said, "No wonder his cousin President Hoover disowned J. Edgar Hoover, because of his hatred."

Well, Millie wasn't looking for that, she was only wanting to see if he had an obituary written as to his family who was left to mourn his death, and she found his loved ones very well listed upon his death.

> Herbert Clark Hoover (August 10, 1874– October 20, 1964). He was a mining engineer, public-spirited, U.S. Secretary of Commerce, and 31st President of the United States, was the son of Jesse Hoover, a blacksmith, and Hulda Minthorn Hoover, a seamstress and a documented minister in the Society of Friends. Hoover was born in West Branch, Iowa. He left Iowa in November 1885, going to Oregon to live with his maternal uncle, Henry-Minthorn.
> https://www.biography.com/people/herbert-hoover-9343371

Hoover lived with his uncle for six years, and left school at the age of 14, to work as a clerk in his uncle's real estate business. Three years later, having decided to pursue a career in engineering, and applied to attend Leland Stanford Junior University, in 1891. He worked hard by doing extracurricular activities, serving as student body treasurer and as manager of both the baseball and football teams.

Millie's roots came from a family of slaves, and her grandfather Big Daddy's father was an offspring of a slave owner, although it was incest, which wasn't uncommon in those days. Yet, Millie found her grandfather's recorded documented obituary, who was an offspring of the slave women Emily, who was a black man born 1893, and other Big Daddy, born just two years before J. Edgar, and his obituary show his family information, military, and friends who were left to mourn his loss.

J. Edgar Hoover's parents and siblings birth and death information:

J. Edgar Hoover's parents and siblings birth and death information	
Dickerson Naylor Hoover	1856-1921
Anna Marie Hoover	1860-1938
Dickerson Naylor Hoover	1880-1944
Lillian Hoover	1881-1959

They all died before J. Edgar Hoover, but were not listed on his obituary, and he had nieces and nephews left to mourn him. Below are allegations that came directly from the Allen family's oral history that accused or was repeated at family reunions regarding J. Edgar Hoover?

- ➤ J. Edgar Hoover's half-sister Mozilla Allen was murdered by orders from J. Edgar Hoover at a young age of 31, leaving five children without a mother.
- ➤ His biological father was Ivery Hoover, and he was murdered by orders from his son J. Edgar Hoover at the young age of 42.

- ➤ He caused a fire in the 1890 census records trying to erase the documents that connected him to the Allen family in Mississippi. This bad deed didn't just hurt our family, but millions of families all over the USA that are now trying to find their roots.
- ➤ He threatened the Allen family to keep his secret of being part black.
- ➤ J. Edgar Hoover made sure that Millie's family had knowledge of the two murders that had already occurred; they would have the same results if his secret were revealed.
- ➤ Dickerson N. Hoover Sr. J. Edgar's white step-father was so angry when he discovered his wife's affair with Ivery Hoover and conceived a child (J. Edgar Hoover). A child with black blood, even with the knowledge he could say the child was his, and he refused to embrace the child as his own throughout his life. Although J. Edgar Hoover tried his entire life to be the son Dickerson N. Hoover wanted with his drive to be the best at his job, but he had to accept the realization that Dickerson was a proud white-man who would never receive a bastard child as his own.

> ➢ Longing to be accepted by his white-step-father Dickerson, J. Edgar allowed himself to be pressured into trying to destroy all the census records that he thought could reveal the secret. He had to make sure none of the "Negros" would live to talk of his secret, so two were murdered to make a point.

> ➢ J. Edgar Hoover purposely and strategically set out to befriended many people who were considered powerful or came into public office just to find out their dark secrets to use if needed in the future. These were actresses, singers, presidents, and most importantly, the Allen family. He would search and dig for negative information/dirt on them and compile private files for his protection and leverage going forward.

Millie final research confirmed all the stories "Big Daddy" told her were indeed the absolute truth. Millie kept her mouth closed for over 61 years with J. Edgar Hoover's dark secret. Now, the life and death of J. Edgar Hoover is an open book.

Our ancestor's needs have been met, and they are set free from the suffering. "Rest in Peace now, Uncle Ivery Hoover, and Mozilla." Millie said.

Chapter 13

LIVINGWITH A SECRET

Many people back in the day and even today live with secrets about crossing the color-line. However, Millie's family was living with many secrets from the time her Big Daddy was born in 1893. They live in fear of being killed if they ever spoke of the many secrets. For many years she thought it was just about J. Edgar Hoover's secret, but it was more than that, it was about the two murders, the sexual abuse during slavery with three slave women, and the ultimate death-threats to Millie's family.

What about "Passing for White?" Passing for white occurs when a person classified as a member of the black race in this instance and is accepted as a member of the white race to live a better life in the 1800s. Historically, the term "Passing for White" was used primarily in the United States to describe Black people who assimilated themselves into the White Race. If the person passing for White were found out, they could be killed or put in jail, which is why J. Edgar Hoover lived in fear his entire life.

Many people did it trying to survive, and many of Millie's family passed for white and never looked back. Millie is still looking for members of her family that passed for white, just as Anna, Elizabeth, and J. Edgar did, living with a secret.

Robert S. Stuckert, a sociologist from Ohio State University, did extensive work using the analysis with census records, which was his demographic information. He estimates that more than three-quarters of all African-American have some white ancestry and at least twenty three percent of all white Americans have an African-American element in their background.

In one of the few statistical studies done on the topic of passing for white, the researchers in sociology and anthropology discovered that as many as 155,000 African-Americans passed for white between 1940 and 1950. It was during the time the Hoovers were intermingling with the Allen slave women and making babies together. So, if those numbers are correct, there are more people than we know now are living under the code of passing for white in America.

How Did People Pass?

Most people didn't know that hundreds of thousands of people changed their racial identity in the1800's. When they did, they didn't just stay in the same house with the same family, in the same neighborhood and keep the same name. They would relocate their family, change their names and mislead a few people on their vital statistics. They would have had to protect themselves.

However, there is a difference today that started in the early 1900s; were blacks are marrying white and vice versa. Millie's said that her children, grandchildren are not passing, but they are marrying into a mixed race, and she loves it because it's not about the skin color that is important to Millie, but, "It's your *character* that is your profound beginning into life."

Our efforts here are to inspire you to do your family research, finding your roots. In doing so, you will, as we have, see that genealogy and the documents you find are essential to your family heritage.

Crossing the color-line

The term **color-line** was first used as a reference to the racial segregation that existed in the United States after the abolishment of slavery. Frederick Douglas's titled, "The Color Line" was published in 1881.

The impact of Brown vs. Board of Education was a law of great need because of its intentions for helping the people. It was on May 17, 1954, when the Court stripped away constitutional sanctions for segregation by race. Today it's called an equal opportunity in education law. However, what was the origin of the need to have such a law? The answer was, Slavery! Then, there was the U.S. Supreme Court's decision regarding, "Brown vs. Board of Education," marked a turning point in the history of race relations in the United States. Now we need more to be done for all the people because many people were forced to cross the color line during slavery.

In the slave families, oral stories of history were the only way they could hold on to a sense of family. Slaves were often separated, and most were not taught to read. Oral family history tradition comes from our ancestors, passed down through generations, which is our cultural tradition that goes back thousands of years.

Millie believed there was another Underground Railroad after finishing her family research. Most people think of the Underground Railroad as a systemic guided routine to get African Americans to freedom. Everyone believed that both white people and black people helped the slaves to freedom, but Millie didn't find any documents proving that the light-skinned people were white and not offspring slave children passing as white people. What if this was a system that the African Americans cooked up to free themselves using the light-skinned, blue-eyed mulatto blacks to help them find freedom. Most of us in the African American community know of relatives who have chosen to pass for white. Some even disowned their relatives to be able to live a better life as a white person.

Millie tells the story about her teacher who passed for white when she went downtown to purchase better school supplies for the colored students that she was teaching. She had blue eyes, and her skin was as white as any white person. This teacher was named Mrs. O'Neal, Millie's teacher at Burglund High School. Millie said she believed she was a white lady until she saw her husband, who was a black man.

Millie remembers studying in her school about the Underground Railroad. The Underground Railroad was a network of secret mapped out directions to safe houses established in the United States during the early to mid-19th century. This system was used to help African-American slaves to escape slavery into free places, such as; Canada and Nova Scotia with the aid of abolitionists, and allies who were sympathetic to their cause.

In Millie's mind, after finishing her researching and studying about the light-skin-blue-eyes colored people, she wondered about the "other" Underground Railroad for the people "Passing for White." Millie talked about her belief that not all of the relationships between whites and blacks were abusive during slavery, since this research. Just as the whites on the plantation had to know of the light-skin-blue-eyes blacks who offered assistance to the dark-skin-brown-eyes blacks trying to escape slavery. They sympathetically helped light-skinned African-Americans who were in the process of crossing color barriers, who were the slave owner's offspring and our historical research proves this point. Millie was always involved in History during her school days and remembers the walkout at school with her entire class because during school vacation Brenda Travis a 16-year-old was arrested. There were five other people with her for being at the city's whites-only Greyhound bus station. When school reopened in October, Brenda was expelled from school. She was sent to reform school and released on parole as long as she left Mississippi within 24 hours. Many students were outraged and walked out of school in protest for the way she was treated, and she was only 16 years old.

Millie also remembers being in a summer camp program, and four of the students were selected to go and stage a sit-in at the Woolworth Department story food counter. They had a lunch counter that refused to serve Black people. Millie was only 16 years old, and she didn't tell her parent she was selected. When she sat at the counter a big white man got up and stood over them smoking his cigar. The students felt intimidated and threatened. He walked over behind Millie and spat in the top of her head, call her the "N" word, and then put his cigar out in the top of her head into his saliva. Millie said she cried, but couldn't tell her parent until she was all grown up.

Millie loved studying about Harriet Tubman and the Underground Railroad and said it helped her connect to her ancestor's spirit. Millie loves Harriet Tubman's quotes, and this one the most, "I never ran my train off the track, and I never lost a passenger." Millie encourages her young students to visit her museum.

"Harriet Tubman was a deeply spiritual woman who lived her ideals and dedicated her life to freedom. She is the Underground Railroad's best-known conductor and before the Civil War. She repeatedly risked her life to guide nearly 70 enslaved people north to find a new life to freedom. https://www.nps.gov/hatu/planyourvisit/index.htm

The Conclusion from the Author

First, let me say how grateful I am to all of those who believed in me, stepped-up to help me finish this journey. Many were shocked to hear about the oral stories and to see their great-great grandfather's name in my research. Kristy said, "I've always believed that my family was as far away as you can get from ever owning slaves."

I am thankful they welcomed me into their home in Seattle, Washington. Then Kristy and her daughter Haley came to visit me at my home in California. I felt like they were family coming to visit, and we took pictures, traveled to Mississippi to visit the Hoover Plantation. We laughed and had fun, which you can see in the final research in this book.

150

My ultimate desire and purpose for my readers are that they find this book inspiring, educational, and attain a better understanding of what a race of people taken away from their home in Africa enslaved for many decades, but still should be treated as a human being.

Remembering my life at ten years old was still quite frightening deep down into my soul when learning of J. Edgar Hoover's secret and how my family was threatened to keep his secrets that caused me great pain back in those days. However, I felt compelled to do this research, which would take 21 years to find evidence and documentation that proved without a shadow of a doubt the stories my grandfather and mother told me were indeed the truth. I was determined to seek out all the facts surrounding J. Edgar Hoover. I wanted to find out why he felt he needed to make outlandish attempts to destroy so many people. The sheer evilness that was within his nature and the horrible accusations he is accused of within our family did make me feel his actions revealed much more than him being born with black blood. These were the actions of a very distort and sinister person.

I am happy to share my roots with my children, and now I am sharing it with you, my readers. This research was inspiring, and at the same time very frightening even though J. Edgar Hoover was dead and gone in 2000. My fear was hurting someone else that would find out that they are related to me, a black woman, and have been living their lives not knowing anything about this history.

However, I wish to say to them, "This work was done to free the spirit of our ancestors, and myself from darkness, and empower others to be brave and tell their truth of family history. I also want to say, remember you can only bear the burden of your deed, the seeds you plant will grow back into your own life."

I wish you all much happiness to the Hoover and Allen families and apologize to anyone that I might have offended in the writing of this book.

I truly believe that God helped me keep those secrets as a child to save my life and I became His helper in freeing the spirits of our ancestors. I was shocked when I didn't find J. Edgar Hoover's birth certificate, even though Big Daddy told me, "You won't find it, because he will erase all of it." I thought I would find his birth record that was filed in 1895 after his birth, but I found exactly what Big Daddy said to be true, he said; "You won't find it, that man doesn't want to be a part of us."

J. Edgar's birth was never filed in 1895, and there was never a birth certificate that was submitted by his parents. He and his half-brother Dickerson N. Hoover Jr. filed his birth record in 1938. I often wonder what kind of threat he gave to Dickerson, and his family to make him do such a thing and falsify legal documents.

In conclusion, I asked God to forgive J. Edgar Hoover for his evil deeds. I came to understand his reasons. Fear of becoming a Black man in those times could have meant immediate death. I am at peace with what he did to my family and others, because forgiveness is good for the soul, and God's Law," which doesn't mean I would ever forget, but I pray that we can learn to love each other as we move forward into the future as "One People."

Thanks to all of you that picked up this book and read my family history on the Allen side. Also thanks to my Big Daddy and mother Alberta Allen-McGhee for trusting me with family history secrets. However, it was time to reveal the truth.

Thanks to God for His protection of me over all these years. He covered my mind until it was time to tell these secrets. He kept me safe and guided me through to research my family's history. For this, I am grateful.

Now, these are great memories of my ancestors who lived for me to have a better life. It will always be with me for the rest of my life.

Our research in Mississippi, UT, and Many other states:

Take a look at the:

- ➢ Census documents
- ➢ Marriage Certificates
- ➢ Death Certificates
- ➢ Divorces Records
- ➢ Land recordings

The documents, census records, and pictures of a few of my ancestors in the photo album was a joy for me to find and be able to share with you, my readers. This book is my gift to my family, grandchildren, friends, and to others in hopes of inspiring them to cherish every minute you have with the storytellers and your family history.

A message from Millie to her readers follows.

The photo Album/Documents and Census records will start now. Review the documents, census records, and pictures in the photo album in this book. It Starts Here! Our research in Mississippi, UT, and Many other states: Take a look at the:

> Research and Family Pictures

> Anna Hoover, Dickerson N. Hoover, and J. Edgar Hoover's Pictures

> Marriage Certificates

> Death Certificates

> Divorces Records

> Land recordings

> Census documents

> Family Group List

The documents, census records, and pictures of a few of my ancestors on the following pages was a joy for me to find and be able to share with my readers. This book is a gift to the family, grandchildren, and others in the world with hopes of inspiring them to cherish every minute you have with the storytellers and your family history.

Now, the next few pages are your view into family Album, documents, Photos, and census records.

In 1957, a little African-American girl named Mildred McGhee was told she was related to J. Edgar Hoover. It was a deadly family secret she kept over 60 years due to death threats to her family. The Proof Is Indisputable, using Oral History, Documents, Pictures, and 21 years of research traveling to McComb, MS, New Orleans, LA, Atlanta, GA, Los Angeles, CA, Salt Lake, UT, Little Rock, AR, North and South Carolina, and Washington, DC.

Now, 2 Family's drawn together after seven decades due to family secrets. "J. Edgar Hoover was a Descendent of Mississippi Slaves!"

Photo
Album
Begins...

OUR TEAM OF FAMILY & FRIENDS RESEARCHING FAMILY ORAL HISTORY!

We finally walked on the ground where our ancestors once walked on, and it was great! This was the Day we received an Award from the Mayor of the City of McComb, MS, and this was the Final Research Trip on the Home Land. We traveled to New Orleans and the Mississippi during this trip.

Research travelers: (back) Denise, Lucius, Leslie, Mertine, Haley, and Queen, (front) Danny, Kristy, Millie, and Regina. A group of family members and friends arrived in McComb, Mississippi April 10, 2002, to find more family history. Our first day was spent reviewing the research from archives in many historical libraries around the USA.

"THERE IS SOMETHING ADDICTING ABOUT A SECRET."

_ J. Edgar Hoover

After 21 years of excruciating and mind-boggling digging, we found the truth! True-life evidence of oral stories told to me that validate there was a connection between my family and the Hoover family. The research is complete, and the proof is indisputable!

J. Edgar Hoover (1895-1972)   *Mildred L. McGhee (1947-)*

Above is J. Edgar Hoover in his early teens & Mildred L. McGhee at ten-years-old. They were relatives and were Descendent of Mississippi Slaves!

This is J. Edgar Hoover!

I noticed that he has resemblance of an African-Americans-person, with the genetic characteristics. Now, look below at the young boys, "Who or Which one is "J. Edgar Hoover?"

It appears that the rumor about the five-year-old boy shown here being Dickerson Jr, not J.E, is true! We did found evidence that this boy is not J.E, although he stated in an interview that it was him, however, it is Dickerson Jr., his half-brother

The picture on the left is J. Edgar Hoover. He was about four years old. A copy of this picture was in Millie's mother's photo book, and she told Millie it was J.E. as a child. He was Big Daddy's first cousin.

ANNA HOOVER, WITH HUSBAND, DICKERSON N. HOOVER
AND SON, DICKERSON JR

Pictured above is also the same picture J. Edgar Hoover presented to Curt Gentry to use in his book, *J. Edgar Hoover; The Man and the Secret.* He claimed the little white boy in the picture was him and not Dickerson Jr. It was so crucial to J. Edgar Hoover to make sure people saw him as a white person and not notice his African-American genes.

DICKERSON AND ANNA - AND - J. EDGAR HOOVER AS
A CHILD

Below: *Clarence Allen "Big Daddy" – J. Edgar Hoover*

1ˢᵗ Cousins

1893 - 1967   1895 – 1972

A YOUNG ANNA HOOVER IN THE 1800S, AND AN OLDER ANNA IN THE 1900S - J. EDGAR HOOVER'S MOTHER.

Anna Hoover "Early Years"

Anna Hoover 1900s

These pictures below are William Hoover, (1832) son William Allen and son Clarence Allen; Big Daddy, and they didn't pass for white.

DR. CHRISTIAN **"KIT"** HOOVER UNCLE IVERY HOOVER'S FATHER

DR. CHRISTIAN KIT HOOVER

This is the Mystery Man. Dr. Christian "Kit" Hoover was born in 1840 and died in 1870. He was the Son of Christian Hoover (1796 – 1868) a Judge, Senator, and Minister of Mississippi. They both were laid to rest on the Hoover Plantation near one another.

BIG DADDY'S PARENTS

William Allen (Hoover)   *Wife Elizabeth Allen*   *Big Daddy*

William Allen; the son of William Hoover, but given the surname "Allen" and his wife Elizabeth Haynes Allen, they were the parents of three children, Clarence Allen my "Big Daddy." Florence Allen Washington, and Rosa Allen Cockerham.

"Young actress Shirley Temple, tours the Federal Bureau of Investigation headquarters in Washington, D.C., June 24, 1938."

https://tucson.com/shirley-temple-and-hoover/image_c24477d6-931e-11e3-be14-001a4bcf887a.html

CLYDE TOLSON AND J. EDGAR HOOVER

Author at age 10.

J. Edgar Hoover was never aware of, Little 10 your old Millie who was planted right in the middle of his life for six decades, and had his secrets deep into her memory.

166

These are the pictures found in our mother's collection that she got from Big Daddy and Big Mama's house after their death. J. Edgar Hoover was Big Daddy's first cousin.

TEN-YEAR-OLD GIRL'S BIG DADDY AND BIG MAMA

This is the author's, "Grandparents; Clarence Allen (Big Daddy); and Litta Allen." (Aka Lydia; Big Mama) They were great parents and grandparents! Still loved and missed by so many even today.

THE OFFICIAL MARRIAGE RECORD FOR "BIG DADDY" CLARENCE ALLEN AND LITTA NEAL

Clarence Allen and Litta Neal were married on December 28, 1915. She had to fill out the application for the marriage. Grandmother Lydia had to have spelled her name as Litta Neal. We the grandchildren spelled her name, Lydia. She signed her name in 1915 as Litta; this was a surprise to Millie.

CLARENCE ALLEN (BIG DADDY); AND LITTA ALLEN."
(Aka Lydia; Big Mama)

Big Mama Lydia and Big Daddy, Clarence Allen with?

This was a picture given to Millie by her father after her mother's death. The two people in the picture standing behind Millie's grandparents are unknown to Millie, and this is what she said, "It is so important to family research that you label the back of all of your picture for the generation to come to know who their relatives are when reviewing the picture album."

THE CHILDREN OF BIG DADDY AND BIG MAMA

This is 15 of the 16 children, all born in McComb, MS.

L-R: Ester, Walter, Roberta, Ruth, Alberta, Rose, Lucille, Eula B, Ina, Leonard, Mildred, Clarence Jr., Lillian, Willie Tyree, Vertis…

The author's mother was Alberta, and Roberta shown in the picture was her Twin. They are both deceased.

12 Children with Parents; Big Daddy and Lydia (Litta)

L-R: Ester, Lucille, vertis, Ruth, Clarence Jr., Ina, Roberta, Mildred, Lillian, Alberta. (Back roll) Eula, and Rose.

Who is missing?

Willie Tyree, Mildred, Walter, and Leonard.

MRS. ALBERTA ALLEN-MCGHEE, MOTHER OF THE AUTHOR.

Mrs. Alberta was 18   *This is her with baby Millie!*

Alberta Allen McGhee

Born: August 28, 1925 – December 21, 2010 Place:

McComb, MS.

Child: The author - Millie LePearl McGhee

Born: November 25/26, 1947

Place: McComb, MS.

There is a short story regarding the author's actual birthday that was shared with Facebook friends on Millie's 71st birthday on the 25th of November. It's an extraordinary story about a mother and the date her daughter was born, by the author.

Millie only wishes her mother was here to read this story. Millie wanted to thank all 169 of her Facebook friends that posted a happy birthday greeting for her on her 71st birthday November 25, 2018, and she was so thankful. This story was the little story she told them about her birthdate and her mother before she passed in 2010!

Millie's mother God rest her soul told her that she was born on Thanksgiving Day in 1947, which made her very happy. So, when Millie researched the date for Thanksgiving in 1947, she was surprised to find the 25th was on Wednesday and Thanksgiving was on November 26, 1947. So, Millie had told my mother those facts that she wasn't born on Thanksgiving Day just because of the date on her birth certificate, November 25, 1947.

Well, Millie's mother went on to say,

"Millie, I ought to know when I had a baby, and I was cutting the Thanksgiving Turkey when you wanted to be born."

Well, with that said, Millie decided to leave it at that and kept on celebrating 11/25 as her birthday. Now, just four years ago, when Millie chose to finish her college degree and had to get my high school records, which was not easy since it was in 1965 when she graduated high school and in McComb, Mississippi. Getting my records was hard.

The college Millie was attending was the University of Maryland University College (UMUC) that Millie was attending needed an official transcript from Burglund High School. Millie was so blessed to get it with the help of a dear friend Beverly Bates. She was working at the school when Millie called, and she was happy to help and went downstairs in the basement of the school and found Millie's records. So, she ordered two copies one for UMUC and one for her.

Well, bless Millie's soul, when she read the birthdate for Mildred L. McGhee on her high school records, she was surprised, because her mother was correct. Millie was born on November 26, 1947, according to the school records, and my mother of course. The hospital and vital records made a mistake. Millie felt terrible because she couldn't go and apologize to her mother for not believing what she told her, and believing what she saw on her birth certificate instead. "Well, that just goes to show us that we are all human and do make mistakes." Replied Millie

So, Millie celebrates the 25th and the 26th, as well as Thanksgiving Day :) as her birthday, which means she could get (3) Gifts from her husband :) she said. Millie Just wanted to share that true-story with you.

"I am now the official storyteller in my family, but I haven't noticed anyone that want to take my place as the family's next storyteller. I hope to pass the tradition of storytelling to one of my grandchildren to keep the family history alive."

—Millie L. McGhee-Morris

The birth certificate of author; Millie L. McGhee-Morris

Birth Certificate stated 11/25/1947 was an error, should have
been 11/26/1947. Many errors were made by the census takers when
recording names and dates back in the day.

Rev. Wm McGhee, and Mrs. Alberta Allen McGhee. They were married for 66 years and had ten children. They raised their children in McComb, Mississippi, until they moved to Southern California in 1967 with the help of their daughter/author of this book, Millie L. McGhee-Morris. Mr. Alberta Allen McGhee passed away December 21, 2010, leaving to miss her, a husband, eight children, and more than 70 grand, great-grand, and great-great-grandchildren. She was a beautiful and loving person. She left a note to all her husband, children, and grandchildren that she wrote when she was getting very sick and was losing her mind to that awful disease Alzheimer's. Millie would love to share a few words of that letter here:

"To Husband and Children & grandchildren's:

"My time here is close Jesus is coming for me soon. Please do this for me don't upset me. I don't want no jealousies and hate to come between you all. I love all of you all, but Jesus is my first love I have my hand in his hand..."

The letter is shared on the next page for the grandchildren in the documents part of the photo album page for the grandchildren to see, and Millie hopes they would hear their grandmother's words. Also, for my readers to see how wonderful, thoughtful, and love Jesus, that was our mother in her lifetime. "We Miss Her."

When Millie's mother Alberta Allen McGhee left this world on December 21, 2010, from the complication of abuse in a nursing home in California, and Alzheimer's disease. Millie's sister Lydia found this envelope that had a letter inside addressed to their father, children, and the grandchildren.

Millie believes their mother knew she was on her way home to Jesus and wanted to talk to her family before she left. Many of the grandchildren haven't seen this letter. Lydia made copies for all the children that were still living after her mother passed.

Now, this book, which is Millie's legacy to her family of family history and the letter will be passed on to generations to come of Mother Alberta Allen McGhee's last best wishes in a few words to her family before she had completely lost her mind to that awful Alzheimer's disease.

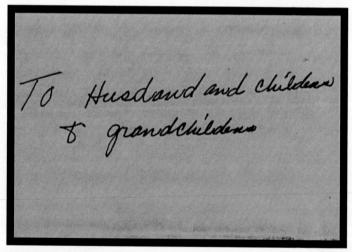

This is the envelope...

The Letter…

To My Husband and Children and grand Children. My time here is Close Jesus is coming for me soon. please do this for me don't up set me. I don want no jealous and Hate to come between you all I love all of you all but Jesus is my great love I have my hand is his Hand.

to My Husband I have try to Make you happy also my Children Mom have did all that I could for you all. Now I want you to give your life to Jesus the man that dil for all of us. and live for him he can't do no more then that for you, and He will Make a way for you. if did any thing to you all please for give me your wife and Mother

Alberta A. McGhee

P.S. hope you can understand what I am trying to said to you all I want you all to Know God is calling for you all also. so get you life in order

This letter is a gift to Mrs. Alberta Allen McGhee's family as "Mother" rest in peace. "What a powerful gift to leave." God loves us, and Jesus wants us to love each other, and forgive. That was her last word to the family.

Death Certificate found of Uncle Ivery Hoover.

Ivery Hoover's Death record, he was born November 24, 1859, and found dead November 18, 1917. This was J. Edgar Hoover's biological father. "He was murdered, due to the threat regarding the secret of his affair with Anna Hoover," said my mother.

Death Certificate found of Malanda Allen-Manning.

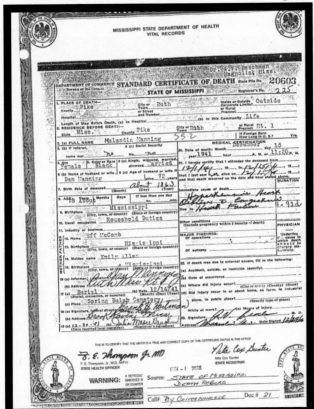

This is the death record of Malanda Allen-Manning who was a slave offspring. Jeff McComb was her father. This was a surprising find for me, which matched the oral history. She is the daughter of Emily Allen slave girl, bed-warmer, daughter/granddaughter, and a cousin of the Hoovers.

Death Certificate found of Florence Allen Washington.

Florence Allen Washington was born on November 13, 1894, and died May 28, 1914, of Typtrnid fever at the age of twenty. It was so exciting to me to find documents that proved my history was real. So many people said I was making this story up, and it was so painful.

We found three death records of people that my mother and my grandfather had told me about, and everything that they told me was in those documents. It was exciting to be able to find Oral History in documents.

This is the Death record of the author's great Aunt Rosa, sister of Big Daddy.

This is the death record of the author's, "Great Aunt Rosa Allen Washington."

Rosa Cockerham was born Dec 3, 1898 in McComb, MS. She died April 9, 1932 at the age of 34 of Post-Operative Shock. My mother told me she had "Alzheimer's" and had run away into the woods. She got lost, and was found dead. Alzheimer's also took my mother in 2010 that is an awful disease that I pray someday will be eradicated. I hope to be a part of donating to the eradication of Alzheimer's someday. Alzheimer's is a disease that takes your mind, and memories of your loved ones.

DOCUMENTS OF CLARENCE ALLEN'S DRAFT REGISTRATION

CARD OF
THE UNITED STATES OF AMERICA.

THIS DOCUMENT STATED THAT CLARENCE ALLEN WAS TALL, THIN, AND HANDSOME.

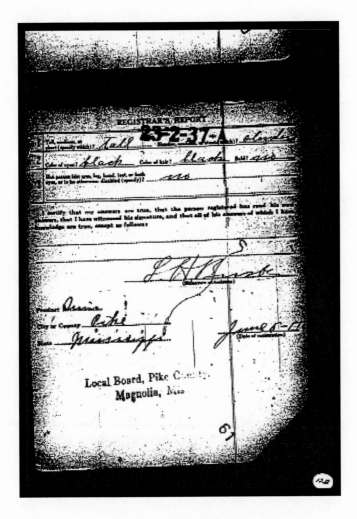

He was a young man, and a United States Citizen.

*During the research we were surprised to find out that they divorced in
1924. (See document below)*

This is a hand written testimony by Lizzie to the State of
Mississippi, pike County, regarding the marriage being dissolved. She
was asking the court to remove his from the premises, and the house
was deeded to her in a divorce.

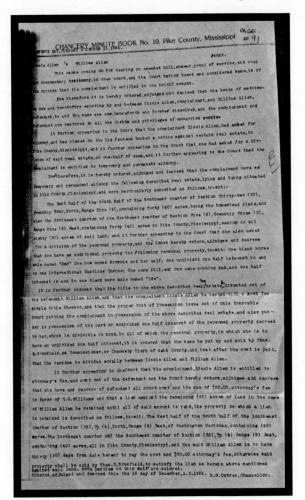

Lizzie Allen vs. William Allen filed #4622 in the Chancery Minute Book No. 10 to adjudged and decreed that the bonds of matrimony dissolved, and they have the rights and privileges of unmarried people, was filed in Pike County, Mississippi on December 16, 1924.

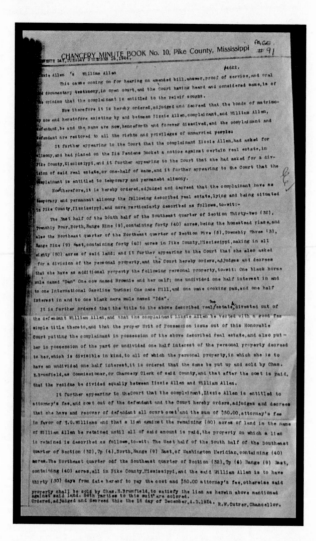

Lizzie Allen vs. William Allen filed #4622 in the Chancery Minute Book No. 10 to adjudged and decreed that the bonds of matrimony dissolved, and they have the rights and privileges of unmarried people, was filed in Pike County, Mississippi on December 16, 1924.

WHAT CENSUS RECORDS LOOKS LIKE:

Above os a 1900 census that shows Dickerson Hoover, with his wife, Anna M., his son Dickerson Jr., age 19, his daughter Lillian, age 17, and a small boy John E., age 5.This was the first time J. Edgar Hoover was recorded in the census records. In checking the 1910 census record in Mississippi, Pike County we found Anna Hoover living in the house with Ivery and his children. She is not found in DC!

This is the 1900 census record of Pike County Mississippi showing Ivery Hoover living with his black wife and their children.

Ten years later we found the 1910 census records in Pike County Mississippi below that shows Ivery Hoover as head of household and husband with his white wife; Anna Hoover...This connects J. Edgar Hoover to his real family, and our oral history that clearly shows us that nothing is really black or white.

The census document above shows in the identification column: W for White, B for Black, and the M for Mulatto," usually the census taker just puts W, B, or M. I'm not sure those are reliable. This record shows William Allen as black and then changed to say he was a White person and not Black.

THE BEGINNING OF THE FOUND BIRTH CERTIFICATE RECORDS FOR J. EDGAR HOOVER...

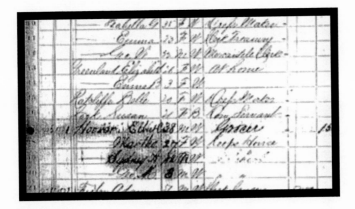

Pictured above is a census records and document that was found erased. This is an erased or tampered record. "J. Edgar Hoover will erase his birth certificate records to hide his connection to us," said Big Daddy. This validates our oral history.

In recording J. Edgar's birth it was obvious it was added some years later, after his actual birth. Page…

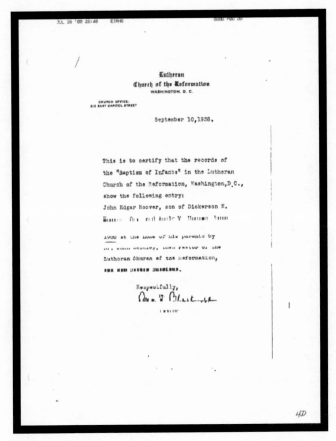

This document reads:

September 10, 1938

This is to certify that the records of the "Baptismof Infants" in the Lutheran Church of the reformation, Washington, D.C., show the following entry: John Edgar Hoover, son of Dickerson N – That is all that is readable.

HEALTH DEPARTMENT, DISTRICT OF COLUMBIA

TRANSCRIPT FROM THE RECORD OF BIRTHS

REPORT OF A BIRTH

Use this form ONLY in case the child BREATHES or shows other evidence of LIFE when the child is altogether outside the mother's body; in other cases use the form provided for the reporting of STILLBIRTHS. If a stillbirth occurs in the practice of a midwife she must report it IMMEDIATELY to the Coroner. This may be done through the nearest police station.

Place of birth .... 413 Seward Square, S. E.   (At Home)
(Give Street and Number)

Full name of child .... JOHN EDGAR HOOVER
(If no name when this report is made, leaves blank until name subsequently added)

Sex of child .... Male   Twins? .... If more than one child was born, state whether
Triplets? .... this report refers to the first, second, or third, etc.
Date of birth .... JANUARY 1st 1895

* Legitimate? Yes. ＿＿＿＿

FATHER	MOTHER
Full name .. Dickerson Naylor Hoover	Maiden name .. Annie Marie Scheitlin
Residence .. 413 Seward Sq., S. E.	Residence .. 413 Seward Square, S. E.
Color .. White .... Age at last birthday 39 yrs.	Color .. White .... Age at last birthday 35 yrs.
Birthplace .. Wash. D. C.	Birthplace .. Wash. D. C.
Occupation .. Government Employee	Occupation .. Housewife

Number of children born to this mother, including present birth .... four (4)
Number of children of this mother now living .... three (3)

CERTIFICATE OF ATTENDING PHYSICIAN OR MIDWIFE

I HEREBY CERTIFY that I attended at the birth of this child, and that it occurred on the
(SEE OVER) .... day of .... 19...... at .... m.,
and that the above information in so far as not based upon my personal observation was furnished
by .... whose relationship to this child is that
of .... and whose address is ....

Signature of ....
(Physican or midwife)

Dated ....   Address ....

Given name .... added from supplemental report .... 19......
*A child is legitimate if either conceived or born in wedlock

REMARKS: (SEE OVER) ....

Correct .. HWH   WASHINGTON, D.C.,   Sept. 21, 1938

The foregoing is a true and correct copy of a certificate of birth filed with the Health Department of
the District of Columbia on .. Sept. 21, ... 19 38 and duly recorded in the records
of said Department.

.... M. D.,
Health Officer, District of Columbia

....
Chief Clerk

(4A)

This document reads:

Report of Birth – Certificate of attending physician or midwife. It showed no physician in attended. This was filed stating, "The foregoing is a true and correct copy of a cerificat of birth filed with the Health Department of the District of Columbia on September 21, 1938. When both parents were deceased.

We also observed a question on the document asking if J. Edgar was "legitimate, Yes or No? The answer selected was No, which meant J. Edgar Hoover was an illegitimate child, just as my oral history stated.

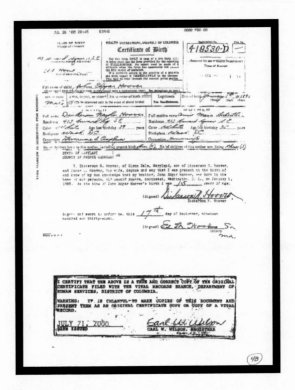

This document reads:

This is the Certificate of Birth that was filed stating, ("The state of Maryland, County of Prince George.")

> "I, Dickerson N. Hoover, of Glenn Dale, Maryland, son of Dickerson N. Hoover, and Annie S. Hoover, depose and say that I was present at the birth of and know of my own knowledge that my brother, John Edgar Hoover, was born in the home of our parents, 413 Seward Square, Southeast, Washington, D.C., on January 1, 1895. At the time of John Edgar Hoover's birth I was 15 years of age." SEAL.

Number of children of this mother now living .... three (3) ....

CERTIFICATE OF ATTENDING PHYSICIAN OR MIDWIFE

I HEREBY CERTIFY that I attended at the birth of this child, and that it occurred on the
(SEE OVER) .... day of ...., 19...... at ....m.
and that the above information in so far as not based upon my personal observation was furnished
by ...., whose relationship to this child is that
of ...., and whose address is ....

Signature of .... (Physician or midwife)

Dated .... Address ....

Given name .... added from supplemental report ....19......

REMARKS: (SEE OVER) ....

Correct. 1895.

WASHINGTON, D.C., ... Sept. 21, 1938

The foregoing is a true and correct copy of a certificate of birth filed with the Health Department of
the District of Columbia on ...... Sept. 21, ... 19 58 and duly recorded in the records
of said Department.

....M. D.
Health Officer, District of Columbia

This document shows:

Below this is showing where there was no doctor when J. Edgar Hoover was born in 1895.

Another view of the birth record that Anna and Dickerson N. Hoover was supposed to file in 1895 with, "The DC Department of Health's Vital Records," but submitted by J. Edgar and his brother in 1938.

A Marriage between Sylvester Bullock and Arie Hoover

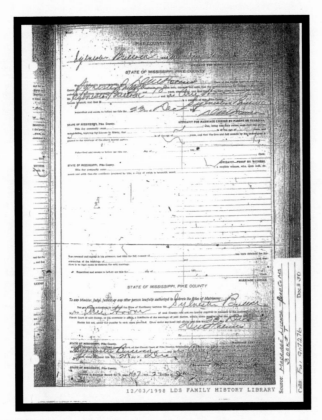

The Marriage License of Sylvester Bullock and Arie Hoover on December 23, 1918. Arie left Ivery/Ivy Hoover after finding out about his affair with J. Edgar Hoover's mother Anna Hoover, and about the birth of a child, "J. Edgar."

ORDER OF SERVICE

Processional: " Nearer My God To Thee"

Hymn: " God Will Take Care Of You"

Scripture: ------------------Appointee

Prayer: ---------------------Appointee

Acknowledgement: --- Mrs. Hattie Sudduth

Solo: ------------ Rev. H. L. Davis

Obituary: --------- Mr. C. D. Higgins

Eulogy: --------- Rev. I. C. Harper

Card of thanks:---- Mrs. Fannie Hampton

Recessional:

CARD OF THANKS

We wish to express our appreciation and gra-
titude for the many expressions of love and
kind deeds extended us during the hours of
bereavement. Thanks to the Ministers for
consoling words and to the Undertaker for
his efficient and courteous service.
The Family

Flower Bearers: Ladies of the Missionary
Society

Pall Bearers: Appointee

Interment: Greenwood Cemetery

People's Funeral Home In Charge

CLARENCE ALLEN (AKA BIG DADDY), (BELOW) IS A COPY OF HIS OBITUARY.

Obituary of, "Clarence Allen."

OBITUARY

We have come together at the call of death, an event that is constantly occuring around us.

Mr. Clarence Allen, Sr. passed away Friday evening 6:40 P.M. August 11, 1967 at his resident.

He was the *son of the* late Mr. William Allen and Mrs. Elizabeth Haynes Allen.

He was born April 9, 1893. He was married to Miss Lydia Neal, and to this union sixteen (16) children were born.

He united with the Summit Baptist Church at an early age. After marriage he moved his membership to the Mt. Zion Baptist Church.

Upon moving to McComb, he united with the Flowery Mount Baptist Church.

He was a retired Carpenter, a loving husband, and a devoted Father.

Survivors are, his wife, Mrs. Lydia Allen, Eleven (11) daughters, Mrs. Lillian Elizabeth Haynes, Mrs. Ruth Knox of McComb, Mississippi Mrs. Mildred Lapearl Varnado, Mrs. Roberta Christmas, Mrs. Lucille Golden, Mrs. Ester Lee Tobias, Mrs. Ina Eugenia Wilson, Mrs. Eula Beatrice Hill, Miss Vertis Lavelle Allen of Chicago, Illinois. Mrs. Rosa Ross Mrs. Alberta McGhee of Los Angeles California.

Four(4) sons, Mr. Willie Tyree Allen of New Orleans, Louiaiana, Mr. Leonard Allen of Washington, D. C. Mr. Walter Allen, and Mr. Clarence Allen , Jr. of Chicago, Illinois. Fifty four(54) Grand children, Two (2) Great Grand children, Two (2) neices, one (1) Nephew. Two foster brothers, Mr. Andrew Williams and Mr. Earl Brooks of New Orleans, Louisiana, and a host of other relatives and friends.

LEGAL DOCUMENT OF CHRISTIAN HOOVER BORN IN 1796. SHOWING HIS MARRIAGE TO HIS VERY YOUNG LOVER AFTER THE DEATH OF HIS FIRST WIFE MARY.

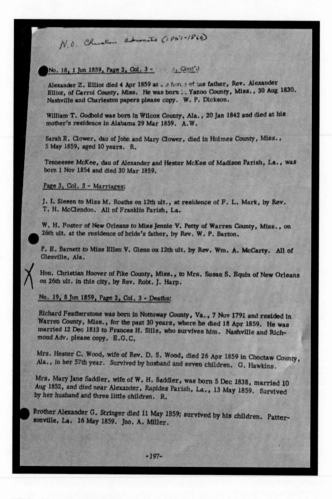

N. O. Christian Advocate (1851-1860)

No. 18, 1 Jun 1859, Page 2, Col. 3 - , Cont'd

Alexander Z. Elliot died 4 Apr 1859 at the home of his father, Rev. Alexander Elliot, of Carrol County, Miss. He was born i. Yazoo County, Miss., 30 Aug 1830. Nashville and Charleston papers please copy. W. P. Dickson.

William T. Godbold was born in Wilcox County, Ala., 20 Jan 1842 and died at his mother's residence in Alabama 29 Mar 1859. A.W.

Sarah E. Clower, dau of John and Mary Clower, died in Holmes County, Miss., 5 May 1859, aged 10 years. R.

Tennessee McKee, dau of Alexander and Hester McKee of Madison Parish, La., was born 1 Nov 1854 and died 30 Mar 1859.

Page 3, Col. 3 - Marriages:

J. I. Siesen to Miss M. Roathe on 12th ult., at residence of F. L. Mark, by Rev. T. H. McClendon. All of Franklin Parish, La.

W. H. Foster of New Orleans to Miss Jennie V. Petty of Warren County, Miss., on 26th ult. at the residence of bride's father, by Rev. W. P. Barton.

P. E. Barnett to Miss Ellen V. Glenn on 12th ult. by Rev. Wm. A. McCarty. All of Glenville, Ala.

Hon. Christian Hoover of Pike County, Miss., to Mrs. Susan S. Equin of New Orleans on 26th ult. in this city, by Rev. Robt. J. Harp.

No. 19, 8 Jun 1859, Page 2, Col. 3 - Deaths:

Richard Featherstone was born in Nottoway County, Va., 7 Nov 1791 and resided in Warren County, Miss., for the past 30 years, where he died 18 Apr 1859. He was married 12 Dec 1813 to Frances H. Sills, who survives him. Nashville and Richmond Adv. please copy. E.G.C.

Mrs. Hester C. Wood, wife of Rev. D. S. Wood, died 26 Apr 1859 in Choctaw County, Ala., in her 57th year. Survived by husband and seven children. G. Hawkins.

Mrs. Mary Jane Saddler, wife of W. H. Saddler, was born 5 Dec 1838, married 10 Aug 1852, and died near Alexander, Rapides Parish, La., 13 May 1859. Survived by her husband and three little children. R.

Brother Alexander G. Stringer died 11 May 1859; survived by his children. Pattersonville, La. 16 May 1859. Jno. A. Miller.

This document reads:

Hon. Christian Hoover of Pike County, Mississippi, married Mrs. Susan S. Equin of New Orleans on the 26th Ult. In this city, by Rev. Robt. J. Harp. (See chapter 4)

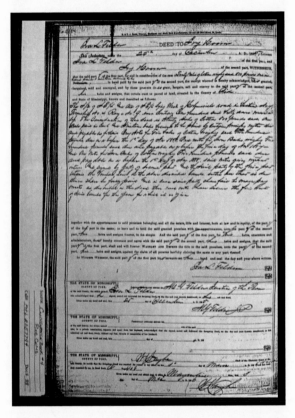

This was an interesting document Millie found in the archives regarding Ivery/Ivy Hoover as he was deeding land to Ira L. Felder in the State of Mississippi, Cunty of Pike. The Conveyane Book #4 Doc# 28. The reason it was interesting was because Millie's mother talk about the Felder family when she was growingup, about a man named Bob, and that's another story. I will never forget that story about a man named "Bob Felder."

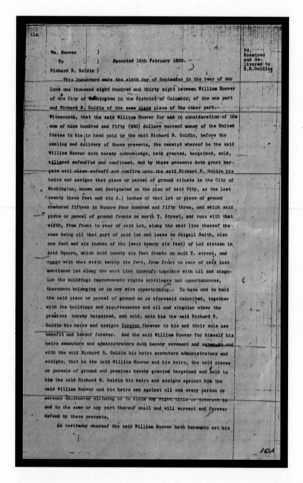

Wm. Hoover)
To) Recorded 18th February 1829. —
Richard R. Goldin)

This Indenture made the sixth day of September in the year of our
Lord one thousand eight hundred and thirty eight between William Hoover
of the City of Washington in the District of Columbia, of the one part
and Richard R. Goldin of the same place place of the other part.—
Witnesseth, that the said William Hoover for and in consideration of the
sum of nine hundred and fifty (950) dollars current money of the United
States to him in hand paid by the said Richard R. Goldin, before the
sealing and delivery of these presents, the receipt whereof he the said
William Hoover doth hereby acknowledge, hath granted, bargained, sold,
aliened enfeoffed and confirmed, and by these presents doth grant bar-
gain sell alien enfeoff and confirm unto the said Richard R. Goldin his
heirs and assigns that piece or parcel of ground situate in the City of
Washington, known and designated on the plan of said City, as the last
twenty three feet and six 6.) inches of that lot or piece of ground
numbered fifteen in Square four hundred and fifty three, and which said
piece or parcel of ground fronts on north T. Street, and runs with that
width, from front to rear of said Lot, along the east line thereof the
same being all that part of said lot not lease to Abigail Smith, also
one foot and six inches of the (west twenty six feet) of Lot sixteen in
said Square, which said twenty six feet fronts on said T. street, and
runs with that width twenty six feet, from front to rear of said last
mentioned lot along the west line thereof; together with all and singular the buildings improvements rights privileges and appurtenances,
thereunto belonging or in any wise appertaining.— To have and to hold
the said piece or parcel of ground so as aforesaid described, together
with the buildings and appurtenances and all and singular other the
premises hereby bargained, and sold, unto him the said Richard R.
Goldin his heirs and assigns forever to his and their sole use
benefit and behoof forever. And the said William Hoover for himself his
heirs executors and administrators doth hereby covenant and agreement and
with the said Richard R. Goldin his heirs executors administrators and
assigns, that he the said William Hoover and his heirs, the said pieces
or parcels of ground and premises hereby granted bargained and sold to
him the said Richard R. Goldin his heirs and assigns against him the
said William Hoover and his heirs and against all and every person or
persons whatsoever claiming or to claim any right title or interest in
and to the same or any part thereof shall and will warrant and forever
defend by these presents,
In testimony whereof the said William Hoover hath hereunto set his

10A

There were four documents discovered with William
Hoover who married Elizabeth Allen doing bargaining deals with
W. Thompson, James Bowen, and Richard R. Goldin. The record
showed Elizabeth now Hoover come into the courtroom and
testified for her husband. It was an interesting document. The
documents stated with 10A, and there were three more 10B,
11A, and 11B found. It may have been so slave trade done this
way in court.

Continuing with document 10B…

hand and affixed his seal the day and year first herein before written.

Signed, sealed and
delivered in the
presence of   William Hoover   (Seal)

Geo. Naylor
James Marshall

District of Columbia,
Washington County, to wit-

Be it known that on this sixth day of September in the year eighteen hundred and thirty eight before the subscribers two of the Justices
of the peace, in and for said County personally appears William Hoover,
the party grantor named in the aforegoing deed, (and known to us as
such) and and acknowledges the same to be his act and deed for the pur-
poses therein expressed, and now at the same time and place also personally appears Mrs. Elizabeth Hoover the wife of the said William Hoover,
and acknowledges the same to be her act and deed- and the said
Elizabeth Hoover being by us privately examined apart from and out of
the presence and hearing of her husband whether she doth make her said
acknowledgment willingly and freely and without being induced to do so
by fear or threats of or ill usage by her husband or fear of his displeasure) she acknowledges and declares that she doth.

Acknowledged before and certified by,

                                        Geo. Naylor, J.P.
                                        James Marshall, J.P.

                        --- 0 ---

Paid Ex-   Corpr. of Washingn.)
amined &   To   )   Recorded 18th February 1839.
delivered
A deliver   A. B. McClean)
-ed to
Grantee   This Indenture, made this 13th day of November in the year of our
2nd
October   Lord one thousand eight hundred and thirty eight between the Mayor,
1840
Board of Aldermen and Board of Common Council of the City of Washington
of the first part, and A. B. McClean of the same place of the second
part: Whereas, the said Corporation, by virtue of the powers in them
vested by their charters have, from time to time laid and imposed
certain annual taxes, on all the real and personal assessable property
within the said City, agreeably to the several assessments thereof, and
have by sundry acts, providing for the collection of such taxes, enact-
ed, "That whenever two or more years taxes on real property, whether
improve or unimproved, in the City of Washington shall remain due and
unpaid; or whenever whenever any special tax, on any real property shall
remain unpaid for two or more years, after the same shall have become
due, it shall be the duty of the Collector in whose hands such taxes

10B

Continuing with document 11A…

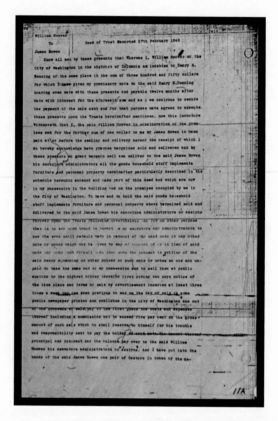

A great document discovered showing some of the dealings with William Hoover, who married Elizabeth Allen, and she passed for white in Washington DC. According to the Oral History records found in our family group records shows her as Christian Hoover slave offspring with the 16-year-old Sarah that was brought from West Africa and sold as a slave.

Continuing with document 11B…

livery of the whole of the articles hereinbefore bargained sold and described in the said schedule.

In Testimony Whereof I have hereunto set my hand and seal this twentieth day of February eighteen hundred and forty three.

Witness   William Hoover   [seal]

W. Thompson

Schedule referred to in the foregoing deed of Trust.

1. sideboard, 2 breakfast & 3 dining tables, 6 cane seat chairs, one rocking chair, 1 doz. common chairs 1 mantle glass, 3 carpets, passage and stair carpets and rods, 1 pair spittons, 1 sett andirons shovel and tongs, 1 candle stand, 1 workstand, 1 crib and bedding, 1 small looking glass, 2 toilet glass, 7 window curtains, 4 feather beds, 4 under beds, and bedding for same, 4 bedsteads 1 trundle do, 3 cupboards, 1 toilet stand, 1 air tight stove, 1 cooking stove, 1 Bureau, 1 kitchen table, 1 washstand, 1 bell metal kettle, 1 wash pot, 1 dinner pot, 2 ovens, 2 skillets, 1 saucepan, 7 grocer boxes, 1 pair of flat irons, 1 clothes horse, 1 coffee mill, 1 teakettle, 5 washing tubs, 40 books of different kinds, 1 doz. stone jars, 6 pitchers & tea sett, 2 doz. dining plates, 10 breakfast plates, 2 doz. breakfast plates, 2 doz. cups and saucers, 2 large dishes, 1 castor cellery glass, 1 doz. table spoons, 1 doz. tea spoons, 1 doz. knives & forks, 4 small waiters, 1 tea board, 2 wooden water buckets, 2 brittania tea pots, 1 coffee pot, & tin boiler, wash bowl & pitcher, 2 market baskets, 3 candlesticks, 1 churn, 1 grocery basket, 3 dripping pans, 6 window frames, 4 sash, 2 door frames, 1 carry all and harness 1 gray horse.

District of Columbia } to wit:
County of Washington }

On this twentieth day of february in the year of our Lord eighteen hundred and forty three, personally appears before the subscriber a Justice of the peace in and for the said County William Hoover and acknowledges the foregoing instrument of writing to be his act and deed according to the true true intent purport and meaning thereof and the act of assembly in such case made & provided.

Acknowledged before & certified by.

W. Thompson   J.P.

11B

Ivey Hoover   To Deed   Ira. L. Felder.

State of Mississippi, County of Pike;

In consideration of the sum of One Dollar to me each in hand paid and the further consideration of the return to me of all the Notes given by myself to I.L. Felder dated Dec.25th,1885 for the land lying in said County and State, described as South half of Southeast ¼ and all that part of South east ¼ that lies west of the Holmesville road in Section 7, in Township 4 of Range 9, conTaining 150 acres more or less, The deed for which recorded Book A, page 408, records of said County. I hereby convey and warrant to the said I.L. Felder the land above described.

Witness my signature this 3 day of January ,1910.
                                    his
                              Ivey X Hoover.
                                   mark.

The State of Mississippi, County of Pike;

Before the undersigned authority in and for said County and State, this day personally came the above named Ivey Hoover, who acknowledged that he signed and delivered the foregoing instrument on the day of the date thereof, as his act and deed.

Witness my hand this 3 day of Jan.1910.

                              E.Y.Howell. J.P.

Filed for record January 4th,1910 at 10 A.M.

Recorded January 11th,1910. W.C.Vaught, Clerk.

Simmons & Boyd & H.H.Simmons   To Deed   N.O.G.N.R.R.Co.

This document is Uncle Ivery signing a legal document with his mark X, he was a businessman but illiterate.

A LEGAL DOCUMENT PERTAINING TO MILLIE'S GREAT-GRANDFATHER WILLIAM ALLEN

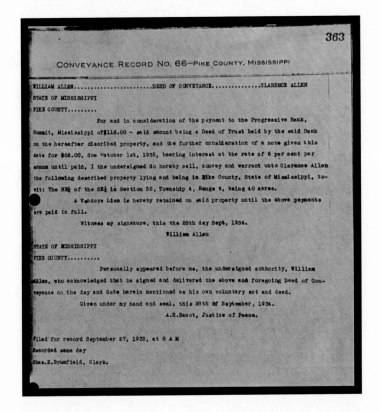

Document reads:

This was a surprise to Millie. William Allen divorced his wife and living with Big Daddy in the State of Mississippi. This is a deed of conveyance was witnessed by Clarence Allen "Big Daddy," for a loan to his father in the amount of $118.00, September 28, 1934 being intrusted from a bank against the land section 32, Townshhip 4, Range 9, being 40 Acres. The note was set to start to be paid October 1, 1935 in the amount of $82.00 one year later.

STARTING THE FAMILY GROUP RECORD
WILLIAM HOOVER AND ELIZABETH

THEY HAD SEVEN CHILDREN

Family Group Record		Page 1 of 2

Husband WILLIAM HOOVER

		Place
Born	Abt 1804	MARYLAND
Christened		Place
Died	1882/1885	Place WASHINGTON, DISTRICT OF COL.
Buried		Place
Married	6 Oct 1832	Place WASHINGTON, DIST OF COLUMBIA

Husband's father MICHAEL HOOVER ?   ☐ Deceased
Husband's mother BARBARA?   ☐ Deceased

Wife ELIZABETH A. HUFF

		Place
Born	Abt 1814	VIRGINIA
Christened		Place
Died	1880/1882	Place WASHINGTON, DISTRICT OF COL.
Buried		Place

Wife's father
Given name(s)   Last name   ☐ Deceased
Wife's mother
Given name(s)   Maiden name   ☐ Deceased

Children List each child in order of birth.

1 Sex M **JOHN T. HOOVER**

		Place
Born	5 Nov 1834	WASHINGTON, DIST OF COLUMBIA
Christened		Place
Died	25 May 1878	Place WASHINGTON, DIST OF COLUMBIA
Buried		Place ROCK CREEK CEM., WASHINTON, DIST OF COLUMBIA
Spouse	CECELIA JANE NAYLOR	
Married	19 Dec 1855	Place WASHINGTON, DIST OF COLUMBIA

2 Sex F **FANNIE HOOVER**

		Place
Born	Abt 1838	WASHINGTON, DIST OF COLUMBIA
Christened		Place
Died		Place
Buried		Place
Spouse		
Married		Place

3 Sex F **INDIANA HOOVER**

		Place
Born	Abt 1840	WASHINGTON, DIST OF COLUMBIA
Christened		Place
Died		Place
Buried		Place
Spouse		
Married		Place

MILLIE'S ORAL HISTORY STATED ELIZABETH WAS THE DAUGHTER OF THE SIXTEEN YEAR OLD SLAVE GIRL FROM WEST AFRICA.

The Oral Story stated:

Elizabeth came from the Allen Plantation in Mississippi and she was the mother of Emily Allen by her father Mr. Allen. So, Mr. Allen was Emily Allen's father /grandfather. Elizabeth met and married William Hoover born in 1804, and had a son they named John T. Hoover. The documents were discovered substantiated this oral history.

WILLIAM HOOVER 1832 AND EMILY ALLEN FAMILY GROUP RECORD OF EIGHT CHILDREN.

Family Group Record — Page 1 of 2

Husband	**WILLIAM HOOVER (FATHER OF ALL?)**
Born	25 Jan 1832 — Place: PIKE CO., MISSISSIPPI
Christened	Place
Died	14 Jun 1903 — Place: MYRTLE PLACE, PIKE, MISSISSIPPI
Buried	Place
Married	Place
Husband's father	CHRISTIAN HOOVER — ☒ Deceased
Husband's mother	MARY NEYLAND — ☒ Deceased

Wife	**EMILY ALLEN**
Born	Abt 1840 — Place: MISSISSIPPI
Christened	Place
Died	1928/1930 — Place: PIKE CO., MISSISSIPPI
Buried	Place
Wife's father (Given name(s))	Last name — ☐ Deceased
Wife's mother (Given name(s))	Maiden name — ☐ Deceased

Children - List each child in order of birth.

1 M	**IVY (SON OF DR. KIT HOOVER) HOOVER**
Born	24 Nov 1839 — Place: PIKE CO., MISSISSIPPI
Christened	Place
Died	18 Nov 1917 — Place: PIKE CO., MISSISSIPPI
Buried	Place: HOOVER CEM., NR. SUMMIT, PIKE, MISSISSIPPI
Spouse	ARIE
Married	Place

2 F	**MALINDA ALLEN (DAU-EF. MCCOMB)**
Born	Jun 1860 — Place: MISSISSIPPI
Christened	Place
Died	15 Dec 1941 — Place: RUTH, PIKE, MISSISSIPPI
Buried	Place
Spouse	DAVID MANNING
Married	Abt 1891 — Place: PROB. PIKE CO., MISSISSIPPI

3 M	**SIMON ALLEN**
Born	Abt 1862 — Place: MISSISSIPPI
Christened	Place
Died	Place
Buried	Place
Spouse	
Married	Place

The documents and census record that were discovered did substantiated the oral history stories of the Allen family.

Continued...

Family Group Record — Page 1 of 1

Husband	WILLIAM HOOVER (FATHER OF ALL?)	
Wife	EMILY ALLEN	
Children	List each child in order of birth	

EBENEZER ALLEN
- Born: Abt 1864 — Place: MISSISSIPPI
- Christened: Place:
- Died: Aft 1930 — Place: HATTIESBURG?, FORREST, MISSISSIPPI
- Buried: Place:
- Spouse: ESTHER ROMINSON
- Married: 1 Oct 1885 — Place: PIKE CO., MISSISSIPPI

LIZZIE ALLEN
- Born: Abt 1868 — Place: MISSISSIPPI
- Christened: Place:
- Died: Place:
- Buried: Place:
- Spouse:
- Married: Place:

WILLIAM ALLEN
- Born: Feb 1870 — Place: PIKE CO. MISSISSIPPI
- Christened: Place:
- Died: 1947 — Place: PIKE CO. MISSISSIPPI
- Buried: Place: SPRINGHOLLAH CEM, PIKE CO., MISSISSIPPI
- Spouse: ELIZABETH HAYNES
- Married: 27 Dec 1892 — Place: PIKE CO. MISSISSIPPI

HARRISON ALLEN
- Born: Abt 1872 — Place: MISSISSIPPI
- Christened: Place:
- Died: Place:
- Buried: Place:
- Spouse:
- Married: Place:

WALTER ALLEN
- Born: Abt 1875 — Place: MISSISSIPPI
- Christened: Place:
- Died: Place:
- Buried: Place:
- Spouse:
- Married: Place:

The Oral Story stated:

Emily Allen had six children with William Hoover, Ivery Hoover was the father by Christian "Kit" Hoover, and Malinda Allen was the father by Jeff McComb. The documents we discovered substantiated our oral history.

WILLIAM ALLEN (HOOVER) "BIG DADDY'S FATHER AND MOTHER; ELIZABETH HAYNES (AKA LIZZA)

Family Group Record		Page 1 of 1

Husband WILLIAM ALLEN

		Place
Born	Feb 1870	PROB. PIKE CO., MISSISSIPPI
Christened		Place
Died	1937	Place PIKE CO., MISSISSIPPI
Buried		Place SPRINGBEULAH CEM, PIKE CO., MISSISSIPPI
Married	27 Dec 1892	Place PIKE CO., MISSISSIPPI

Husband's father WILLIAM HOOVER (FATHER OF ALL?)   ☒ Deceased

Husband's mother EMILY ALLEN   ☒ Deceased

Wife ELIZABETH HAYNES

		Place
Born	Nov 1870	MISSISSIPPI
Christened		Place
Died	Abt 1941	Place PIKE CO., MISSISSIPPI
Buried		Place MC COMB CEM., MC COMB, PIKE, MISSISSIPPI

Wife's father Given name(s)		Last name	☐ Deceased
Wife's mother Given name(s)		Maiden name	☐ Deceased

Children List each child in order of birth.

1 Sex M **CLARENCE ALLEN**

		Place
X Born	9 Apr 1893	LINCOLN CO., MISSISSIPPI
Christened		Place
Died	Aug 1967	Place PIKE CO., MISSISSIPPI
Buried		Place
Spouse	LETTA NEAL	
Married	26 Dec 1915	Place PIKE CO., MISSISSIPPI

Sex F **FLORENCE ALLEN**

		Place
Born	13 Nov 1894	SUMMIT, PIKE, MISSISSIPPI
Christened		Place
Died	28 May 1914	Place PIKE CO., MISSISSIPPI
Buried		Place
Spouse	MACON WASHINGTON	
Married	2 Mar 1914	Place PIKE CO., MISSISSIPPI

Sex F **ROSA A. ALLEN**

		Place
Born	4 Dec 1896	PIKE CO., MISSISSIPPI
Christened		Place
Died	7 Apr 1932	Place MC COMB, PIKE, MISSISSIPPI
Buried		Place
Spouse	IVORY COCHRUM	
Married		Place

"FAMILY GROUP RECORDS" OF CLARENCE ALLEN (BIG DADDY) OF THE SIXTEEN CHILDREN.

The documents and census record that were discovered did substantiated the oral history stories of the Allen family.

CLARENCE ALLEN AND LITTA'S 16 CHILDREN
CONTINUES...

Family Group Record

Husband	CLARENCE ALLEN	
Wife	LETTA NEAL	

Children List each child in order of birth.

4 F MILDRED ALLEN

		Place
Born	23 Apr 1924	SUMMIT, PIKE, MISSISSIPPI
Christened		Place
Died	21 Aug 1984	CHICAGO, COOK, ILLINOIS
Buried		Place
Spouse	BERNARD "SONNY" LAWRENCE	
Married		Place

5 F ALBERTA ALLEN

		Place
Born	28 Oct 1925	SUMMIT, PIKE, MISSISSIPPI
Christened		Place
Died		Place
Buried		Place
Spouse	WILLIAM A. MC GHEE	
Married	12 Sep 1944	SUMMIT, PIKE, MISSISSIPPI

6 F ROBERTA ALLEN

		Place
Born	28 Oct 1925	SUMMIT, PIKE, MISSISSIPPI
Christened		Place
Died	28 Oct 1999	CHICAGO, COOK, ILLINOIS
Buried		Place
Spouse	CHRISTMAS	
Married		Place

7 F RUTH ALLEN

		Place
Born	1926/1927	SUMMIT, PIKE, MISSISSIPPI
Christened		Place
Died	18 Apr 1988	JACKSON, HINDS, MISSISSIPPI
Buried		Place
Spouse	CHARLES LEE KNOX	
Married	2 Jun 1947	PIKE COUNTY, MISSISSIPPI

8 M WALTER ALLEN

		Place
Born	24 Feb 1928	SUMMIT, PIKE, MISSISSIPPI
Christened		Place
Died	16 Aug 1982	CHICAGO, COOK, ILLINOIS
Buried		Place
Spouse	DOROTHY GARNER	
Married		Place

F LUCILLE ALLEN

		Place
Born	5 Sep 1929	SUMMIT, PIKE, MISSISSIPPI
Christened		Place
Died	3 Apr 2001	CHICAGO, COOK, ILLINOIS
Buried		Place
Spouse	EMANUEL GOLDEN (DIV)	
Married	11 Apr 1947	PIKE COUNTY, MISSISSIPPI

16 Aug 2001

CLARENCE ALLEN AND LITTA'S 16 -CHILDREN CONTINUES!
The documents were discovered that substantiated this oral history.

CONTINUES...

The documents were discovered that substantiated this oral history.

Family Group Record			Page 3 of 3

Husband CLARENCE ALLEN

Wife LETTA NEAL

Children List each child in order of birth.

10 Sex F — **ESTER LEE ALLEN**
Born	16 Dec 1930	Place	SUMMIT, PIKE, MISSISSIPPI
Christened		Place	
Died		Place	
Buried		Place	
Spouse	HARRIS TOBIAS		
Married		Place	

11 Sex F — **ROSA ALLEN**
Born	1932	Place	SUMMIT, PIKE, MISSISSIPPI
Christened		Place	
Died		Place	
Buried		Place	
Spouse	D.C. ROSS		
Married		Place	

12 Sex M — **CLARENCE ALLEN**
Born	Jun 1934	Place	SUMMIT, PIKE, MISSISSIPPI
Christened		Place	
Died		Place	
Buried		Place	
Spouse	VERA		
Married		Place	

13 Sex F — **INA E. ALLEN**
Born	1936-1937	Place	SUMMIT, PIKE, MISSISSIPPI
Christened		Place	
Died		Place	
Buried		Place	
Spouse	JAMES WILSON		
Married		Place	

14 Sex F — **EULA B. ALLEN**
Born	1937-1938	Place	SUMMIT, PIKE, MISSISSIPPI
Christened		Place	
Died		Place	
Buried		Place	
Spouse	ED HILL		
Married		Place	

15 Sex F — **VERTIS ALLEN**
Born	20 Jul 1939	Place	SUMMIT, PIKE, MISSISSIPPI
Christened		Place	
Died		Place	
Buried		Place	
Spouse			
Married		Place	

WILLIAM MCGHEE AND ALBERTA ALLEN-MCGHEE IS MILLIE'S
PARENTS." FAMILY GROUP RECORD "TEN CHILDREN" LISTED.

Family Group Record

Page 1

Husband	WILLIAM A. MC GHEE			
Born		Place		
Christened		Place		
Died		Place		
Buried		Place		
Married	12 Sep 1944	Place SUMMIT, PIKE, MISSISSIPPI		
Husband's father Given name(s)			Last name	☐ Deceased
Husband's mother Given name(s)			Maiden name	☐ Deceased

Wife	ALBERTA ALLEN			
Born	28 Oct 1925	Place SUMMIT, PIKE, MISSISSIPPI		
Christened		Place		
Died		Place		
Buried		Place		
Wife's father	CLARENCE ALLEN			☒ Deceased
Wife's mother	LETTA NEAL			☐ Deceased

Children   List each child in order of birth.

1 Sex F   QUEENESTER MC GHEE

Born	8 Aug 1945	Place SUMMIT, PIKE, MISSISSIPPI
Christened		Place
Died		Place
Buried		Place
Spouse	MC ARTHUR TOBIAS (DIV)	
Married		Place

2 Sex M   WILLIAM L. MC GHEE

Born	12 Dec 1946	Place SUMMIT, PIKE, MISSISSIPPI
Christened		Place
Died		Place
Buried		Place
Spouse	MARIAN HILLS	
Married		Place

3 Sex F   MILDRED PEARL MC GHEE

X	Born	23 Nov 1947	Place SUMMIT, PIKE, MISSISSIPPI
	Christened		Place
	Died		Place
	Buried		Place
	Spouse		
	Married		Place

14 Aug 2001

WILLIAM MCGHEE - ALBERTA ALLEN-MCGHEE FAMILY GROUP RECORD CONTINUES…

Family Group Record — Page 2

| Husband | WILLIAM A. MC GHEE |
| Wife | ALBERTA ALLEN |

Children   List each child in order of birth.

4 M   JAMES EDWARD MC GHEE
Born 16 May 1949   Place SUMMIT, PIKE, MISSISSIPPI
Christened   Place
Died 1949 1950   Place
Buried   Place
Spouse
Married   Place

5 M   DOUGLAS DWAYNE MC GHEE
Born 26 Apr 1950   Place SUMMIT, PIKE, MISSISSIPPI
Christened   Place
Died   Place
Buried   Place
Spouse PRISTINE LUCAS
Married   Place

6 M   BOBBY EUGENE MC GHEE
Born 12 Apr 1951   Place SUMMIT, PIKE, MISSISSIPPI
Christened   Place
Died   Place
Buried   Place
Spouse GWEN (DIV)
Married   Place

7 F   LYDIA MC GHEE
Born 20 Jul 1952   Place SUMMIT, PIKE, MISSISSIPPI
Christened   Place
Died   Place
Buried   Place
Spouse MAURICE MOUTON
Married   Place

8 F   EDDIS MARIE MC GHEE
Born 10 Feb 1954   Place SUMMIT, PIKE, MISSISSIPPI
Christened   Place
Died 1963   Place
Buried   Place
Spouse
Married   Place

9 F   SILVIE ANN MC GHEE
Born 29 Dec 1954   Place SUMMIT, PIKE, MISSISSIPPI
Christened   Place
Died   Place
Buried   Place
Spouse GREGORY THOMAS
Married   Place

16 Aug 2001

Family Group Record — Page 3 of

| Husband | WILLIAM A. MC GHEE |
| Wife | ALBERTA ALLEN |

Children   List each child in order of birth.

10 F   JANETTE MC GHEE
Born 16 Dec 1955   Place SUMMIT, PIKE, MISSISSIPPI
Christened   Place
Died   Place
Buried   Place
Spouse MICHAEL OIDRICH (DIV)
Married   Place

MCCOMB MISSISSIPPI GOVERNMENT PROJECT.

The author, Mildred L. McGhee was born and raised in this Apartment, in McComb, MS!

The address is "[C4 Apartment 1 Utopian Homes, in McComb, Mississippi. The actual apartment in McComb, MS, where she lived, and it is still standing after 70 years of the author's life. She grew up here until she was 17 years old.

THIS IS THE TEN-YEAR-OLD GIRL AT SEVENTEEN HIGH SCHOOL GRADUATION DAY JUNE 2, 1965.

Millie has always wanted to become an author. She loved writing short stories and reading them to her family on special nights during Bible study. She didn't know at that time that she was illiterate, but Millie wrote the words on the paper, and only she could read them.

Rev. Wm McGhee and Mrs. Alberta Allen-McGhee

The very young Rev. and Mrs. McGhee in McComb, MS. They are the parents of Author, Millie L. McGhee-Morris.

The McGhee family in 1965.

Millis's house, in the Government Project looked the same in 2003 as it did in 1947 when Millie was born.. In the picture is her parents and eight of the children, Millis had left and moved to California. A brother had died as a baby, leaving eight children living at this time. The children in the picture are Queen, Bill Jr., Douglas, Lydia, Bobby, Sylvia, and Jeannette.

Millie was sixteen years old, still living in the government projects. She's dressed for church with her family.

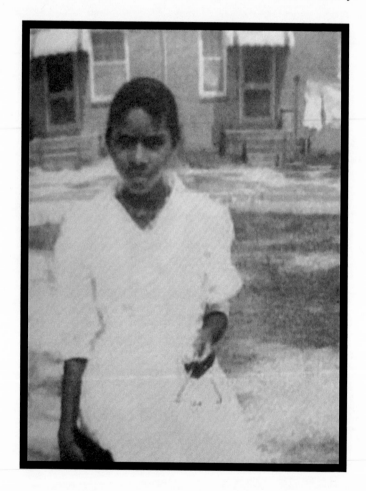

Danny, he is Hispanic and came into Millie's life during this research. He volunteered his time to travel with me and help find her roots. Danny became Millie Godson and had stayed in her lives since 2000. It's a great story about the life of Millie and Danny. They changed each other's life for the better, and remain Mom Millie and godson Danny.

"The McGhee children's Christmas, when they were young."

It's Millie's parents Mrs. Alberta Allen-McGhee and Rev. William McGhee's home on Christmas Day. The toys the girls always received in a shoebox, which was a little black-doll and a little white doll. Millie's father said, "I wanted you all to know that human beings come in minute shapes and colors. The white/black dolls represented the equivalent of all people, like flowers of all different colors, but yet they are still flowers."

A Great Man, who loved his family.

Millie and her godfather; the late Johnnie L. Cochran Sr. He was so proud of her for the work she was doing finding her roots. He encouraged Millie to get her best education and follow her dreams. Millie loved him so much, and she misses him.

Author at age 10.

Author, Millie L. McGhee-Morris

The ten-year-old girl, who kept the family secrets until a time to tell, and freed her ancestors, as well as herself. Now, she can move into her life in peace living her passion. She did her DNA.

DNA Test for Author, Millie L. McGhee-Morris Listed as Mildred L. Morris legal name on record. African Ancestry Here by Certifies that Mildred L. Morris Shares Maternal Genetic Ancestry with:

The Djola people living in Guinea-Bissau, West Africa.
Based on a MatriClan analysis performed on
December 19, 2008
Signed by: Rick Kittles, Ph.D.
Scientific Director

Millie said,
"It was like looking in mirror at my family in Guinea – Bissau in West Africa"
Millie's DNA Report:

These are Millie's people. "It's my Family, and I wish to meet them someday." said Millie. Like looking in a Mirror!

The parents of 10 children.

In the picture below is; father is eating watermelon, Brother Bobby standing behind Millie, and Lydia next to Millie and Brother Douglas on the other side. The two little girls are Sylvia and Jeannette.

Millie's Big Daddy's big white house Millie visited as a child. They were playing in the yard. In the picture is "Big Daddy sitting on the porch and Millie's sister Queen and Bill Jr. standing behind Millie. Millie was about 5years old.

A Dream Come True.

Millie had never been inside the City Hall in McComb, Mississippi. When she lived in McComb, segregation was explicit. "Blacks lived on one side of the railroad tracks, and the White's lived on the other side.

Millie is in her study mood, and she sees a surname of a Mayor that showed up in her family history. "McComb!" Jeff McComb fathered one of Emily's children, "Melinda Allen."

Colonel Henry Simpson McComb. Millie found in Genealogy that **Henry Simpson McComb** was born in 1825, and died in 1881. His family tree on Genie, with over 185 million profiles of ancestors and living relatives.

Artwork by LaTasha Tobias

A family tree designed that was by another Niece named LaTasha Tobias. She is very talented. She drew this family tree and placed the Allen family on one side, and the Hoover's on the other side.

A great analogy, however, the tree is rooted in the ground. The tree sprouts out branches and leaves; however, they all belong together as a family. All are coming from the same root!

This is Millie's father; Rev. Wm McGhee in California talking with Mrs. King.

Mrs. Coretta Scott King and Rev. William A McGhee, Millie's father, had an extraordinary time at Second Baptist Church Los Angeles, CA talking about living in the South. About 30 years ago! Millie met her that day and told her that she reminded her of her mother, Alberta. "A beautiful Lady."

Millie remembered being in the Martin Luther King movement in McComb, Mississippi at her god-father's home, and later his home was bombed. Millie had a chance to meet Mrs. Coretta Scott King, and loved the book written about her inspiring life by Dr. Barbara Reynolds called, My Life –My Love – My Legacy.

"DID THE ALLEN AND HOOVER FAMILY LOOK ALIKE?" CHECK OUT J. EDGAR HOOVER, CLARENCE ALLEN SR., AND JR. PICTURES BELOW:

J. Edgar Hoover

Clarence Allen Sr.

J. Edgar Hoover

Clarence Allen Jr.

J. Edgar Hoover

Clarence Allen Jr.

Millie's Hoover cousin and her daughter in Mississippi visiting
City Hall with Millie.

Millie in conversation with Mayor J.C Woods of
McComb, Mississippi in 2002, and received an award for her
work.

K106 Radio broadcast in McComb, Mississippi.

Millie arrived at K106 preparing for a radio talk show that aired in McComb, Washington, and California. She met and loved speaking with Carl. Much love and thanks to the late Carl Lazenby. A sweet man who showed Millie a lot of respect and love at the radio station. May he rest in peace!

Millie and Brother Lucius Bowser. He would be so proud of Millie for never giving up, and Tamela Tenpenny-Lewis for assisting in finishing what the team at AAHGS Arkansas started together.

Tamela Tenpenny-Lewis
Genealogist/Historian/Cemetery Preservationist
Co-founder, Preservation of African American Cemeteries, Inc. past National President, (AAHGS) Afro-American Historical & Genealogical Society, Inc.

The Mississippi Trip! "Hello, Lucius Bowser." Always reading. – New Orleans, Louisiana. Millie always said, "Lucius is passing for Black." All in FUN! He is missed!

Author, Millie McGhee and Historian and genealogist traveled with me for over ten years. They were best friends, and Millie misses him, and she knows he is smiling down at her right now because he believed in Millie. "Rest in Peace Lue."

Millie on the air in McComb, Mississippi, with
Wallace Allen –Westside Story Newspaper

Millie and her sister Queen visiting their first home before
moving to the Government Projects in McComb, MS.

This is Mayor J. C. Woods of McComb, MS and a dear friend Jacqueline Martin who Millie grow up with in McComb. She was the Administrator of the Mayor's office

This is Author, Millie, and her cousin Kristy Hoover Sullivan meeting the Mayor, J. C. Woods. This was Millie's first time in City Hall in 2003.

Millie was on radio with Fern Crossley in Mississippi.

Millie's trip to Salt Lake City Utah with her team George and his Assistant Ted. Millie spent two weeks with them going through the most extensive genealogy Library in the country. She collected documents of census records, death records, and birth records on her family. Then, Mr. Larry Carroll, a news journalist joined us, and we traveled to many other states, Atlanta, Louisiana, and Mississippi looking for records.

Big Daddy and his two sisters, Rosa and Florence Allen.

This is Clarence Allen the grandson and granddaughters of
William Hoover (1832) and J. Edgar Hoover's first cousin.

Rev/ Wm McGhee at work at the Time Newspaper in California in 1960s. He Married Mrs. Alberta Allen the daughter of Clarence Allen (Hoover) of McComb, MS.

A Document about 16 sixteen-year-old Sarah Allen.

We had been looking for Sarah on the Hoover plantation since Elizabeth was born. Sarah was brought from her home in West Africa and given the name Allen because she was purchased as a slave and owned by Mr. Allen in Mississippi, a good friend of the Hoovers.

COUSINS

Kristy Hoover Sullivan & Millie L. McGhee

They first met in California.

Kristy Hoover Sullivan & Millie L. McGhee

Our time together was special and fun!

It was an exhilarating day; the way Kristy and Millie met was priceless. Millie's newfound cousin Kristy Hoover Sullivan emailed her after a family member found Millie's book of research about the Allen's and the Hoovers in "Secrets Uncovered, J. Edgar Hoover Passing for White?"

Kristy said, "I feel like I'm looking into a mirror," when she met my mother, and my mother said she liked just like the Hoovers in the family. Millie wanted to bond with her new found cousin and took the time doing just that, and it was exciting to Millie.

Kristy was in town for a conference, and Millie traveled to see her with a lot of the family research. Millie said they must have gone through those documents and my book for hours. Kristy couldn't believe her family had anything to do with owning slaves.

There are more pictures in the book of journey with Millie's team, and you will see how they were like one people, nobody was thinking "White or Black" it was just a family fun time going through documents, the graveyards, churches, restaurants, looking at the places our ancestors may have lived, and going through family stories. They even went to the Mall shopping together, and it was a lot of fun.

Now Review the Mississippi Trip research…

The next few pages will take you through some of the travel of finding my roots...

Pictures of Author Millie L. McGhee-Morris and her group of "Researchers in MD in 2003, with her new found Hoover Family. "Millie and Kristy family forever!"

Kristy

Millie

Lucius Bowsers Historian

Cookie our "Police Office"

Mertine Moore Brown "PR "

Millie and mother the story tellers. Research in mccomb, mississippi. Our team of researchers, "millie's mother, husband, friend, family and members of the hoover family!"

Millie and cousin Kristy "BFF   *Millie's sister Queen*

A WALK THROUGH THE ANCESTORS AND

DESCENDANTS RESTING PLACE...

THE MYSTERY MAN, IVERY HOOVER, WAS J. EDGAR HOOVER'S BIOLOGICAL FATHER

Born: November 24, 1859 - November 18, 1917.

The Mississippi Trip helped us find the connection to the oral stories. We found J. Edgar Hoover's biological father's resting place here on the Hoover's Plantation. The research team felt this was a connection to the Hoover family. The death record of Ivery Hoover showed the researchers his father as, Dr. Christian Kit Hoover.

The researchers was an exciting find in researching family history, and it was the key to the Allen and Hoover's family history.

J. Edgar Hoover was born in Washington, D.C. He served as director of the United States Federal Bureau of Investigation Chief for over forty eight years until his death.
His Burial place was: Congressional Cemetery
Washington, Death: 2 May 1972 (aged 77) Washington, D.C. Plot: Range 20, Site 117

Clyde Anderson Tolson was a lifetime companion of J. Edgar Hoover.
He was buried close by.

252

Clyde Anderson Tolson gravesite was close to J. Edgar Hoover's.

He was born May 22, 1900, and died April 14, 1975, three years after J. Edgar Hoover.

Annie M., Sadie M., and Dickerson N. Hoover
Congressional Cemetery

Sadie M. Hoover was only three years old when she died. She was born in 1890, five years before J. Edgar Hoover in 1895.

Dickerson Naylor Hoover Jr

Dickerson Naylor Hoover Jr., was born, September 9, 1880. In the District of Columbia, USA, and he died October 22, 1944. His Burial was at Fort Lincoln Cemetery in Brentwood, Prince George's County, Maryland, USA. Memorial ID 79452832

No gravesite for Dickerson's daughter;

Lillian Hoover Robinette

Born November 12, 1881, and died July 5, 1956 at the age of 74. Her burial was Cremated, Ashes given to family or friends.

Sadie Marguerite Hoover

Born June 2, 1890, and died August 2, 1893, she was only 3-years-old. Her burial ground was in the same plot with Anna Hoover and Dickerson N. Hoover in the Congressional Cemetery, Washington D.C.

There were three blue candles left by an anonymous person on June 9, 2018

One for Dickerson who died long before I was born, and one for J. Edgar, a fine man that I'll never forget, and for Miss Helen, the keeper of treasures…

"This was an interesting piece of history. When I read it, it made me think of a love one who were looking into his/her family tree, and remembering. Also, that we came from a different side of the tree. I send her my love." _Millie

(See the pictures of our journey together below)

Mississippi Trip to review research with J.E. Hoover's claimed relatives... April 2002

"The Bogue Chitto Grave Site."

THE HOOVER PLANTATION GRAVE SITE LOCATED ON THE
PLANTATION. WE FOUND IVERY HOOVER,
"Bogue Chitto"

THE HOOVER PLANTATION GRAVE SITE LOCATED ON
THE PLANTATION. WE FOUND IVERY HOOVER.

Ivery Hoover (1859 - 1917)

Author visits the Grave Site in McComb, giving special time, and love to her grandparents. "Clarence & Lydia Allen."
Summit Pike County, Mississippi

This is the gravesite of Millie's Hero her Big Daddy. Summit Pike County, Mississippi

My sister "Re Re" Eddis Marie McGhee, the author's sister who
died at twelve years old. February 10, 1954 - 1965

*This is the gravesite of Big Daddy's 1st Son, Willie Tyre
"Jack Allen" 1918-1974*

Dear Readers:

I wanted to share the reviews on Amazon regarding the first time I tried to tell this secret. I didn't know that I wasn't ready to write a book about this amazing story. I needed to reach out to others to help me, so I was still trying to keep this entire story inside and wrote the story like fiction or make-believe.

Now, reading these reviews that are still on Amazon regarding the book I called, Secret Uncovered, J. Edgar Hoover passing for white? I hadn't finished my research into the entire story, and I believe in my heart I was still afraid to tell the whole truth. I wasn't ready to say this fantastic, shocking, fearful, and true story of a family who lived through slavery.

I want to thank all of the people for their reading the book, and those who thought it was mostly just an imaginary story, such as Patsy Butler, who gave me 1 star, because she was expecting the real true story. I thank her for her review because it gave me the strength to do more in finding all of the missing pieces in the archives. I also want to thank the others who respected my effort and gave me 4 to 5 stars. It was all of you that gave me hope that I could find the documents to match my oral storytelling history given to me by my grandfather and a wonderful mother.

Let me say this before my new readers read the reviews from the published book in 2000. Many of them are correct because I had not finished the research. It was my first book, and most of all I did write it like a fantasy, or an imaginary novel. I think I was still afraid of telling the real truth regarding the pain my ancestors had to endure, and most of all I didn't know what to do with my fear that was still in my soul.

I tried to tell this story in 2000. I didn't know the magnitude of what had been given to me in 1957. I didn't have a clue of how to break-down and decipher the documents or write a book of this extent. However, in reading the reviews that I have placed in the last pages of this book helped me, I realized I had a lot more work to do.

These are the <u>unedited</u> reviews from the book that was released in 2000 on Amazon.

5.0 out of 5 stars
Thank God Someone told this story!
August 22, 2000

L. Ericson

"I have lived for more than forty-five years with my own secret, and Secrets Uncovered put me at peace in revealing and dealing with my own ancestry. My mother is white, and after my father's death as a teenager, I went on to pass for white. I never had children for fear my secret would be found, and have always felt guilty about this. But now I can at last come forward with pride, and let the world know of my own mixed bloodline. Your book also shed new light on a different side of the slave/master relationship, and it was tender to hear of the love between Master Hoover and your Great Grandmother. Thank you for sharing this story, and also thank you for shedding light on the true ancestry of J. Edgar Hoover. Now many things are more clear about his racial hatred and actions, and I hope the world will see his hypocracy. Also your book reminds us that there are many out there like Hoover and I, and hopefully future mixed generations of all races will not feel the shame of their blended bloodlines. I can now honestly say that I do not." Thank you, Ms. McGhee.

5.0 out of 5 stars

A New and INTERESTING Way To Learn History!
January 25, 2001

"This book was very interesting and allowed me to enjoy history... I did not think I would find a book about history that I could actually enjoy... Millie you have proved me wrong and I thank you for that... Got any more stories about your past??? If so e-mail me this young person is interested! You have led an interesting life and you are soo very loved by many... I'm probably one of your biggest fans and I know you will be getting that alot... But whether you believe me or not I know in my heart it is true... I too want to join in the line of erasing the colored line because it pains me to look around and see how many outcast people due to race... my dad is one of them and I totally hate it! I LOVE PEOPLE and I hope that people love me for my heart and soul not for what color I am because God made us all in his Image... We are all children of God... Love and Christ, Just another person in this world tryin to make a difference!"

Chie Smith

4.0 out of 5 stars

264

When your Black your Black!
November 29, 2000

"Millie McGee has written a pivotal and thought provoking book. I was very eager to get started on her book after meeting Millie through a dear mutual friend and remembered that she said she was writing a book about her lineage. The information on J. Edgar Hoover was intriguing. The underground passage for "passing white" was new information. The book was well written and researched and had me anticipating each page.Her book has also inspired me to continue my own writings on my lineage as well. I find this new information on J. Edgar Hoover interesting and would like to read other books written about him."

Judith C. Damewood

5.0 out of 5 stars

Slave times, Oral Traditions and J. Edgar Hoover
June 30, 2000

Format: Paperback
"The author of this fascinating book grew up listening to stories of her slave ancestor and her white master named Hoover, with whom she had seven children. Convinced that her ancestors were in a loving relationship, she feels impelled to write their story. As she writes, she remembers being told of a possible relationship to J. Edgar Hoover. She delves into her ancestors' past and comes up with intriguing facts and speculations. The author's family story is warm and wonderful as well as somewhat spicy, and provides a different view of slave times than we usually read about. It is her hope that recognizing common backgrounds can help people of various racial backgrounds to minimize their differences and get along. I loved this book."

Kristy L Hoover Sullivan
4.0 out of 5 stars

<u>A letter from home</u>
January 31, 2001

<u>Format: Paperback</u>
"My maiden name is Hoover. Our family story is that we didn't want to claim our foggy relationship to J. Edgar. Millie's book was like a letter from home. I applaud her efforts and courage to enlighten those of us who had no clue about the truth hidden in family secrets while my white lineage took advantage of our priveledges in a white society. Through her work, I've met a long lost cousin and kindled new hope that we can heal another chapter in the sad story of America's race relations.

Knowing this book was a personal accomplishment of a woman who graduated from high school nearly illiterate adds another angle of interest to her work. A fascinating story."

<u>Edith Patterson</u>
4.0 out of 5 stars

<u>Informative</u>
November 27, 2000

<u>Format: Paperback</u>
"Bravo Miss McGhee! Your book solidified what many of us had "heard thru the grapevine" for so long. I was especially impressed with your hometown research and photographs. It answered a lot of questions for me. I could have done without the graphic sexual portrayals, but if that was the way it was honestly revealed to you...well. But on the whole, I believe the book was well researched and hopefully gave others a hunger to further research the complicated man named Hoover."

BOOK CLUB QUESTIONS...

1. What did you feel while reading this book?

2. What were the feelings you got about the ten year old girl keeping that secret?

3. How different was these two families history from yours the readers?

4. What did you think about J. Edgar Hoover's birth records?

5. Did this book inspire you? If not, why?

6. Why do you think this research took 21 years to complete?

7. What do you think about the author?

8. Did Big Daddy make a mistake telling the author the secret?

9. What did you feel about Sarah, Elizabeth and Emily?

10. What did you think about the white women?

THE AUTHOR AND HER HUSBAND

Dr. Leslie and Millie McGhee-Morris

Married April 14, 1990 in Las Vegas, Nevada